Home Economics Instruction
in the Secondary Schools

THE LIBRARY OF EDUCATION

A Project of The Center for Applied Research in Education, Inc.

G. R. Gottschalk, Director

Categories of Coverage

I	II	III
Curriculum and Teaching	Administration, Organization, and Finance	Psychology for Educators

IV	V	VI
History, Philosophy, and Social Foundations	Professional Skills	Educational Institutions

Home Economics Instruction
in the Secondary Schools

BEULAH I. COON

The Center for Applied Research in Education, Inc.
New York

Second Printing... May, 1966

LIBRARY OF CONGRESS
CATALOG CARD NO.: 64–11024

PRINTED IN THE UNITED STATES OF AMERICA

Foreword

Teachers and school administrators who read this book will gain a vivid perspective of the historic and contemporary purposes of home economics education. Many readers will be impressed by the foresight of the pioneers in a field which closely affects the health and well-being of everyone and by the author's challenges for inventing and adapting curriculum and programs to the scientific changes of these times. The teacher of home economics will experience a new sense of the significance of her work; the administrator will realize the importance of providing the support and facilities to attract and hold teachers who are successful in this area of instruction. Both teachers and administrators will have a clearer concept of the urgency to step up the schools' role in strengthening family, home, and community life.

Because of her rich experience and her excellent channels of communication with leaders and practitioners in every part of the country, the author is able to report the best current practices, current needs, and major trends. Moreover, she focuses attention realistically on the relation of home economics to the total curriculum and the over-all objectives of the school.

In addition to specific and practical ideas on curriculum building and instruction, this book offers the reader some suggestions for planning, remodeling, and equipping centers for home economics. The reader has the advantage of being able to draw on the best practices the country affords and to avoid the costly mistakes of others. By applying the principles delineated in this book, administrators and teachers can develop functional home economics centers provided with the most suitable learning aids and adapted to the special requirements of pupils and communities.

The reader will discover that the distinctive feature of this book is its combination of practicality and imaginative applications. The practical but creative ideas found in every chapter will be beneficial to *all* teachers. Finally, the book deals forthrightly with the whole problem of teacher preparation within the context of a modern program of home economics.

Here is a book which might well be read by all teachers and certainly by all administrators. To them it will give a new appreciation of home economics as a dynamic approach for strengthening family life, improving physical and mental health, and adding to the daily enjoyment of living in a complex, scientific, and automated society.

LAWRENCE G. DERTHICK
Assistant Executive Secretary
for Educational Services
National Education Association

Home Economics Instruction
in the Secondary Schools

Beulah I. Coon

Miss Coon's book on *Home Economics Instruction in the Secondary Schools* is one of a group in the Library of Education Series treating specialized subjects at the high school level. The vocational subjects form an area of their own within this group. The volume by Miss Coon is parallel to *Business Education,* by Dr. Lloyd V. Douglas, which has already been published in the Library of Education, and to certain other volumes presently in preparation.

Miss Coon writes from a background of a long period of study and experience in the field of secondary school home economics. Her book treats the historical development of home economics as a school subject, and the relation of this development to social and technological changes in the society. Careful attention is given to the modern organization of the curriculum in home economics, with illustrations drawn from programs actually in effect in several states. Methods of teaching home economics are discussed in relation to the psychological principles of learning, rather than on the subject matter to be taught, the methods of teaching, or the teacher; each of these topics is treated in terms of the ultimate effect on the young people who are to study home economics in the high school. The entire book is characterized by the practicality of the suggestions offered for the program of home economics in the modern secondary school.

JOHN DALE RUSSELL
Content Editor

Contents

Home Economics Instruction
in the Secondary Schools

CHAPTER I

Purposes and Outcomes
of Home Economics Instruction

Home economics, an area of education focused on the individual and on family living, has been affected by those social, economic, and scientific changes in the American environment which have had an impact on home living. Its chief development as a subject of instruction in the public schools occurred during this century, although there was some instruction in certain phases of the subject in the last quarter of the nineteenth century. The content then was largely determined by the aims of the manual training movement— "to train the mind, eye, and hand to work in unison"—and the emphasis was on those skills which involved the use of the hands. But during the last half of the nineteenth century many leaders urged that schools include as a part of their program the scientific, social, and economic study of the home in order that "the next generation may live on a higher plane than the present one."

One group whose influence was a potent factor in changing the purpose from that of manual training to the study of home and family was the Lake Placid Conference, meeting first in 1899. The name was derived from Lake Placid, New York, where the conference met each year for ten years. Its concern, at the turn of the century, was with the education of girls. The group (which, in 1909, formed the American Home Economics Association) suggested the name *home economics* and at the third conference, in 1901, declared:

> The ultimate aim of such instruction is to give the girl a realizing sense of her responsibilities; to make her feel that it is just as necessary to place the house on a scientific basis as the farm; that whether she be wife, mother, or sister, she is largely responsible for existing conditions and atmosphere of the home; that on her rests the decision of the problems as to whether the home shall be the place

1

wherein each member shall reach his or her highest physical, intellectual, and spiritual development.[1]

Concepts of Home Economics

The report of the sixth annual conference of the Lake Placid group (1904) included a broader definition of home economics:

Home economics stands for
The ideal home life of today unhampered by traditions of the past.
The utilization of all resources of modern science to improve the home life.
The freedom of the home from the dominance of things and their due subordination to ideals.
The simplicity in material surroundings which will most free the spirit for the more important and permanent interests of the home and of society.[2]

Through the years, many other definitions have been given. The most recent, formulated in 1959 by The Philosophy and Objectives Committee of the American Home Economics Association, stated:

Home economics is the field of knowledge and service primarily concerned with strengthening family life through:
educating the individual for family living
improving the services and goods used by families
conducting research to discover the changing needs of individuals and the means of satisfying these needs
furthering community, national, and world conditions favorable to family living
Home economics synthesizes knowledge drawn from its own research, from the physical, biological, and social sciences and the arts and applies this knowledge to improving the lives of families and individuals. Its concern is with these aspects of family living:
family relationships and child development
consumption and other economic aspects of personal and family living
nutritional needs and the selection, preservation, preparation, and use of food
design, selection, construction, and care of clothing, and its psychological and social significance

---

[1] Lake Placid Conferences on Home Economics, *Proceedings of the Third Conference* (Lake Placid, N.Y., 1901), p. 53.
[2] Lake Placid Conference on Home Economics, *Proceedings of the Sixth Conference* (Lake Placid, N.Y., 1904), p. 31.

textiles for clothing and for the home

housing for the family and equipment and furnishings for the household

art as an integral part of everyday life

management in the use of resources so that the values and goals of the individual, the family, or of society may be attained.[3]

A comparison of the emphasis in the early 1900's and that in 1959 indicates agreement on the close relationship between the sciences and their application to the home and family. The 1959 statement gives more recognition to the contribution of art and the social sciences and to such aspects as family relationships, child development, and the psychological and social significance of clothing, thus reflecting changes in society, increased knowledge from research in psychology, and a growing interdependence of individuals, families, and society. The 1959 statement considers the individual and the family rather than focusing attention solely on the education of the girl. The shift in focus is another recognition of the changes which have occurred in the roles of the various family members.

The Importance of Education for Home Living

The statements made by the Lake Placid Conference members and by most of the committees and leaders in the field since the turn of the century agree that home economics should focus primarily on strengthening the home by developing in students the ability to live constructively at home and with the family.

The importance of such a goal has been recognized by many people in education and by people from many other disciplines. As early as 1918, worthy home membership was listed as one of the seven cardinal principles of secondary school education.[4] The purpose of the 1941 Yearbook of the American Association of School Administrators, *Education for Family Life,* was "to give impetus to a movement already begun, to develop a more general consciousness of the importance of training for family life as a responsibility

---

[3] The Committee on Philosophy and Objectives of Home Economics, *Home Economics New Directions* (Washington, D.C.: American Home Economics Association, 1959), pp. 4–5.

[4] National Education Association Commission on the Reorganization of Secondary Education, *Cardinal Principles of Secondary Education,* U.S. Dept. of Interior, Bureau of Education, Bulletin No. 35 (Washington, D.C.: USGPO, 1918).

of public education."[5] Among the goals cited in *Behavioral Goals of General Education in High School* (1957) are appreciation of the home, conservation of family ideals, skill in homemaking, maintenance of democratic family relationships, consumer judgment and efficiency in buying, and consumer protection.[6]

All who realize the vital place of the family in American society would be likely to agree that education for family living cannot be left to chance. According to the Panel on Education and the Future of America:

> It is essential for us to understand that the tone of our daily lives profoundly affects the quality of our society and it is essential to recognize that of all factors involved in establishing that tone the family is the most important.[7]

Overstreet emphasizes a similar idea:

> No social institution is more fateful for the human race than the home. In it the primary shaping of character takes place. In a good home, maturing gets quickly underway: the child is helped to grow from stage to stage of confidence, skill, affection, responsibility, and understanding.[8]

Bernice Moore, after a study of data collected from 13,000 high school students in Texas, concluded that one does not automatically acquire the ability to establish and maintain a home:

> Capacities for family living and skills for homemaking have to be studied and learned. This is no less true than that future scientific and technological achievement rests upon an educational base.[9]

Summarizing letters from 10,000 young mothers, Hunt reported that nine out of ten faced many—often serious—frustrations and difficulties, among which were uncertainty in dealing with children;

---

[5] American Association of School Administrators Commission on Education for Family Life, *Education for Family Life* (Washington, D.C.: National Education Association, 1941), p. 11.

[6] Will French and Associates, *Behavioral Goals of General Education in High School* (New York: Russell Sage Foundation, 1957), pp. 58–62.

[7] The Rockefeller Report on Education, *The Pursuit of Excellence,* Panel Report V, America at Midcentury Series (Garden City, N.Y.: Doubleday & Company, Inc., 1958), p. 19.

[8] Harry A. Overstreet, *The Mature Mind* (New York: W. W. Norton & Company, Inc., 1949), p. 230.

[9] Bernice Milburn Moore, *The Case for Education for Home and Family Living,* based on findings of the Texas Cooperative Youth Study (Austin, Texas: The University of Texas, 1962), p. 3. Mimeographed.

difficulty in organizing housework so as not to become a slave to it; problems in handling and managing money; and inability to control responses to the multitude of demands from their husbands, their children, their friends, their community, and their own inner selves.[10] It has become increasingly important for secondary school pupils to be given some preparation for solving these problems, particularly in light of the rise in teen-age marriages.

To establish and maintain the quality of family life which is necessary in the second half of the twentieth century calls for knowledge not in existence a few years ago. Traditional solutions are not adaptable to the kinds of decisions which have to be made in modern family living. In a dynamic society such as ours, it is at least as important to focus new insights from psychology, natural science, economics, and sociology on homemaking as it is to focus them on other occupations and professions. Few learn to be wise parents and constructive family members as an incidental outcome of living.

No one aspect of the school's program can provide the education which insures satisfactory family life. In fact, such education is a concern of the school, the home, the church, and the community, for families unable to make satisfactory adjustments hamper the development of the community and the nation. It is important, however, that one part of the school program should focus on this aspect of daily living.

Purposes of Home Economics

What, then, are the purposes of education for family living? Some are common to all education; for example, to help pupils to think critically and creatively, to clarify their values, to broaden and deepen their interests, to help them develop a philosophy of life. Other purposes are unique to home economics teachers, although supported by contributions from other subject fields. In trying to achieve these purposes, pupils study certain aspects of family living: child development, family and social relations, management of resources, consumer competence, food and nutrition, clothing and textiles, housing, and family health.

To understand the importance to society of families in which

---

[10] Morton M. Hunt, "How 10,000 Young Mothers Feel about Their Marriages, Their Children, Themselves," *Redbook* (September, 1961), 29–31, 82–86.

each individual has an opportunity to develop his optimum po-
tential—physically, socially, intellectually, emotionally. Achieving this goal involves an understanding that individuals differ in
physique, in social development, in intellectual capacity, in emotional stability, and in potential, and that a democratic society is
enhanced if these unique capacities are developed. In trying to understand why individuals differ, pupils come to realize the extent
to which families differ in what they value, in what they become,
and in what they can contribute to society.

Although many people subconsciously recognize the potent influence which the home and the family exert on individuals, the
extent of that power and its effects throughout life have either not
become a conscious part of the thinking of many individuals or
else have not served as a guide to making their contributions constructive. Evidence of this is found in the apologetic statement so
many women make: "I'm just a homemaker"; in the lack of whole-
some influences in the homes of youth and adults involved in de-
linquency and crime; in the serious emotional problems found in
children who come from broken homes. Another type of evidence
comes from research indicating that inadequate nutrition of teen-
age girls affects the health of their children; that poor food habits
at any economic or age level have serious health consequences; and
that crowded housing and insufficient or unbecoming clothing may
result in illness, in lack of social participation, and in emotional
problems.

First, the potential contribution of the family to the individual
and to society must be recognized. The influences on the family
exerted by institutions outside the home must also be understood.
Industry, business, the church, the school, and all the media of
mass communication are constantly affecting the various members
of the family. Some of the influences are very constructive and
helpful; others—such as inadequate or uncertain income, group
tensions, intolerance, and corruption—may be so serious as to keep
homes insecure or even to destroy them.[11]

This goal of understanding the interdependence and interrelationships between the home and society should underlie all teaching
of home economics. Special attention to this objective should be

---

[11] Overstreet, *op. cit.,* pp. 232–39.

given in the aspects of home economics concerned with child development, family-community relations, management, and consumer education. Young people need help if they are to understand what is involved in establishing and maintaining a home which is an asset to society. They need to understand the necessary factors for satisfying family and social relationships. They need to become aware of their own and their family's values and the ways in which these values influence their decisions. They need help in interpreting the potent influences on their own lives: both the constructive and the destructive contributions of families to society, and the influences and pressures exerted on the family by forces outside the home. They can become aware then of the different values and goals held by other individuals and families and the influence these values and goals have on the way others live. These interrelationships between the family and the community can be made clear whenever various community services (such as family welfare, child welfare, education, recreation, housing, and shopping services) are evaluated. Of equal importance is the concrete help pupils can gain in understanding themselves and their relations with their peers, their family, and their friends.

To understand some of the satisfactions and needs the individual has as he participates in the various stages of the family life cycle. To become better able to guide their own development and that of their children, young people need help in understanding the process of human development, the kind of behavior which can be expected at different stages in a person's development, and the varying rates of growth among individuals. It is important that they come to realize that each stage of development has its special opportunities and problems and that it is difficult to achieve full development in the later stages if some aspects of growth have been arrested in the earlier stages. What, then, are the basic needs of infants? of preschool children? of primary school children? of pre-adolescent youth? How may these be satisfactorily met? What are likely to be the needs of adolescents? of young adults? of young parents? of parents whose children have left home? of the aging? How may these different needs be met?

As teachers help pupils in their study of child development, they seek to develop in them an understanding of the emotional, social, and physical needs of children and some ability to meet these needs.

As pupils observe children and try to understand the differences they see, they begin to get more understanding of themselves as adolescents. Through their study of social relations, friendships, and relations between parents and children, they come to understand better some of the later stages of human development. A study of factors to consider in establishing a family has come to be important to many high school students. It is vital that young people be helped to understand their emotional attitudes and to set standards for their personal relationships. The increase in average life span also brings problems as well as satisfactions to individuals and families, for careful planning is necessary if adequate provision is to be made for the housing, nutrition, social, and health needs of the aging.

Some of the questions which home economics pupils would study in relation to these problems are: What are some of the health problems of young children? How are these met today as contrasted with several years ago? What are the family's responsibilities in relation to them? What is the effect of love and emotional security on the development of the infant and the child? What provisions may be made for children whose mothers have to work? What facilities does the community already have and what new facilities does it need to assist parents in the care of children? What are some of the factors which make for a successful marriage and for a happy family life? What facilities are available for marriage counseling? What is needed for the growing proportion of aged citizens? To what extent is aging a family concern and to what extent is it a community concern?

To understand and be able to apply some of the important concepts, principles, and generalizations in home economics, in the sciences, and in the arts which are basic to family living. Rapid changes affecting family living continuously result in new problems to be solved and situations to be met. It has long been impossible to learn all the facts which might be needed for future living. But research has indicated that learning is more permanent when the learner understands the concepts, principles, or generalizations involved. Instead of the rapid rate of forgetting which usually occurs when detailed facts are learned, understanding tends to grow when concepts and generalizations have been found to apply in several situations. Whatever the aspect of home economics with which pupils are concerned, the teacher should ask herself: [12] What generalizations are important to the pupils to make them independent in new situations and what kinds of experiences are needed to help pupils recognize how widely these generalizations may apply. Sometimes these generalizations will be developed in home economics classes, sometimes in science, art, or social science classes. In any case, the experiences in home economics classes will usually be those which make apparent the application of these generalizations to the home.

As pupils are studying child development and watching the reactions of different children to similar situations and similar kinds of guidance, they sense that individuals differ appreciably in their reactions. If they are able to visit children in their homes, it may become even more apparent that there are personal and environmental reasons for these differences. Gradually they come to understand that behavior is caused. Progressing from the idea "This child is bad" to "I wonder why this child reacts as he does" may make a real difference in their contacts with their own younger brothers and sisters as well as with other children. Many will begin to see evidence of this truth in themselves and gain a greater understanding of why they react as they do. The author recalls vividly one senior high school boy in a home economics class who had spent three days visiting a nursery school. His report of the relation between the children and the nursery school teacher's calm, permissive, friendly guidance clearly indicated that this was his first realization that an adult-child relationship might be democratic instead of authoritarian. The author's impression was that this experience was so meaningful it would be likely to make a real difference in the boy's concept of himself as a father.

Another illustration may indicate the way in which pupils come to generalize and then to see the applications of the generalization. A pupil's question about a specific cleaning agent she had seen advertised on television led class members to collect advertisements of this and similar products, to try out the products, and then to analyze the facts given and the appeals made for these products. They found that the differences among the products were minor, that the number of facts given was limited, and concluded that the appeals

---

[12] The feminine gender has been used because, to date, most secondary school teachers of home economics are women.

were primarily emotional. But they observed that costs per unit differed. This led them to study advertisements for other products and their costs. They realized they needed sources of information other than advertising and found advantages and disadvantages in different sources. This led to a comparison of costs of other articles and the conclusion that price is not necessarily indicative of quality, and for some products may be influenced by quantity purchased.

Some facility in performing certain tasks necessary for the maintenance of a home and family. This facility can add to young people's sense of achievement and make possible better management of their time and energy. Although recognized and dominant in many early courses, this goal assumes much less importance in modern home living. Many goods and services formerly produced or performed at home are so generally available outside at similar cost, or so much more easily and quickly performed with the equipment many modern homes have, that it is no longer justifiable for most pupils to spend an appreciable amount of school time developing these manipulative skills.

However, some of the manipulative skills—such as caring for food, for clothing, for the house and its equipment and furnishings; preparing, serving, and preserving food; and constructing and repairing clothing—will need to be considered. Some pupils will find enjoyment in performing certain of the manual skills and will want to use them in creative activities. Others will want to perform them only when they are economically profitable and time permits.

Whenever a skill is taught, it is important to analyze the steps to be taken, the time- and energy-saving procedures to be used, and the reasons for which they are used. It is also necessary to repeat the tasks so that each of the steps is accurately learned. A high degree of skill can be attained only with much time for practice, and much of this practice will have to take place in the home rather than in the school.

When pupils are learning to perform a task, they should be helped to understand the principles involved in the process so that they are in a position to analyze the difficulties encountered and to learn how to overcome them. In preparing food, for example, there are easy and desirable ways to pare a potato, to fold in a beaten egg white, to care for the working surface. An understanding of the nutrients which lie just under the skin of fruits and vegetables, of the effect of beating on egg white, of the effect of different cleaning agents on specific kinds of working surfaces will help when these tasks are performed later. In cooking food, the principles involved in retaining the nutritive values of different food elements and in achieving an attractive and palatable product should be clearly understood. Similarly, when making a garment, an understanding of the purposes served by specific kinds of seams or finishes provides a basis for making a choice when another garment is made. Many household tasks can be performed intelligently only if the reasons for desirable procedures are clarified. In caring for equipment, an understanding of the principles underlying its operation helps in providing more intelligent care. In storing food, it is important to understand why some kinds must be kept cold, some tightly covered, some dry.

Often, one of the most difficult problems for young homemakers is organization of routine so that tasks may be fitted easily into the time schedule, unnecessary steps eliminated, and sufficient variation in activities planned to avoid undue fatigue. Practice in organizing work in the laboratory, supplemented by planned home experiences, can often suggest patterns which will be helpful when new situations arise.

To become more adept at managing one's own and the family's human and material resources so as to attain one's consciously derived goals and values. This objective involves clarifying one's own goals and values, recognizing the many kinds of resources individuals and families have, considering the possibilities of substituting one resource for another, being able to resolve conflicts among different goals or values, using the scientific method in considering important problems, and making decisions, carrying them out, and evaluating outcomes.

Each individual tends to accept, without much analysis, those values which have been held by his family. He often does not realize the extent to which these values have been shaping his actions and reactions. As the teacher helps him to recognize the reasons for his own actions and to think of the values held by other individuals and families and how these influence their practices, he is in a better position to consider and evaluate the values important to him. This also helps him set goals for himself for immediate and later living.

In making decisions for oneself, the variety of resources involved is often more limited than that involved when a family decision is to be made. One's time, energy, knowledge, skills, abilities, money, and possessions—and one's attitudes about the use of each of these —may be primary considerations. Involved also is consideration of the ways in which the decision may affect others. When decisions involving the family are to be made, attention usually has to be given to the various family members—their values and goals, their time, energy, abilities, and interests in using or developing skills and abilities—as well as to family income and standards and the facilities in the community which may be used in place of, or in addition to, family facilities.

Most decisions have to be made with full recognition of the limitation of such resources as time, energy, money, and present possessions—and also with the realization that if one or more of these is used, it will not be available for a different use. When decisions upon the goal to which the resources are to be allocated are made with these limitations clearly in mind, the individual is prepared to accept the possible disadvantages as well as the satisfactions which follow as a consequence of the decision made. Part of the maturing process with which young people may need help is that of giving thought to long-range goals as well as to immediate outcomes.

Besides helping pupils to prepare for the decision-making process by careful consideration of goals, values, and resources, it is important to help them become conscious of the steps involved in the process of problem-solving, which is so often used in decision-making, so that they will tend to use this process in situations important to themselves and their families. What is the specific problem? What are possible solutions? What are the facts needed about each of the possible solutions in order to make a wise decision? How and where may reliable facts be found? In view of these facts and the values one considers important, what solution will be most satisfying? After a solution has been decided upon and carried out, what were the results? Might another solution be more desirable another time? Experience in carrying through these steps should help pupils to make fewer spur-of-the-moment decisions on important problems.

The complexities of twentieth century living call for an infinite number of managerial decisions. The teacher who recognizes the great importance of managerial ability in home living will be on the alert to opportunities which permit her to develop this ability in her pupils. They will be helped to realize that there is no one decision which is right for all individuals and families, to analyze what they and their families really want, to think through possible ways to attain these goals, to find facts which are pertinent to the problem under consideration, and to evaluate the results of decisions as a basis for later decision-making.

Few choices affect only the individual making them. As already noted, an adolescent girl's choice of food may affect the health of the children she later bears. The ability to distinguish between food fads and food facts can vitally affect the health of the individual and the family. The furniture selected by a young married couple may influence the kinds of restrictions or prohibitions that must be placed later on the activities of their children. Buying a shoddy garment for one occasion is uneconomical, and every purchase helps to determine what retailers think they should stock in the future.

Perhaps the decisions made by the individual as an individual or as a member of a family are the easiest to make and are likely to be given the greatest attention. Those decisions made by citizens and members of groups are likely to be given least attention, yet these decisions are vital to family living for they involve one's sense of values and influence the use of individual and community resources. How are people to be protected from products which are harmful, unsanitary, or falsely advertised? What kind of labelling is needed in order to buy wisely? Do citizens want their tax money to be spent for schools, for roads, or for health? What is UNICEF doing around the world? Does it merit support? How can one give it support? How do decisions and choices in this country differ from those in less well-developed countries or from those in countries with an autocratic system of government? In considering these questions, the home economics teacher and the social studies teacher may well cooperate in helping pupils to understand the issues involved and to develop the ability to make decisions significant to families, to the community, and to the nation.

All these objectives guide the home economics teacher in choosing experiences for her pupils. When the experiences are wisely chosen, each pupil should make significant progress toward these goals; but with the individual differences which exist in any one class, the outcomes will differ with the pupils' interests, abilities, and opportunities for experiences at home and in the community as well as at school.

Some Outcomes of Home Economics

Progress toward each of these goals should be expected in all home economics classes in the secondary school. The outcomes will be seen in various aspects of family living (see pp. 2–3). Many of these outcomes will be subtle evidence of the attitudes, interests, sensitivities, and appreciations which have developed; others will reflect more thoughtful use of resources, sounder decisions, and more constructive contributions to the family and to the community. Results will vary with the type of pupil, his home background, his previous schooling, and the kind and amount of home economics he has studied.

The outcomes given below serve only as illustrations of the many which can be looked for. The secondary school pupil who has studied home economics may be expected:

To be more outgoing and understanding in making new friends and keeping old ones;

To be able to discuss differences with his parents more understandingly and less emotionally;

To enjoy stages in small children's development;

To be better able to give constructive guidance to children;

To make purchases, or resist them, after thoughtful consideration of his own and his family's resources and goals;

To figure the cost of credit from different sources as one basis for deciding whether, if an article must be purchased on the installment plan, it is worth the cost;

To select food which meets nutritional needs;

To plan a meal which can be prepared with the time and money available;

To choose a garment, with the money available, which enhances the wearer and is suitable to the occasion for which it will be worn;

To select a tool or piece of equipment after deciding the qualities and standards desired and investigating the extent to which those available meet these criteria;

To be interested in becoming acquainted with people who have a background different from his own;

To appreciate the contributions made to individuals by families with values and customs different from his own;

To understand some of the problems and difficulties of families or individuals with very limited incomes;

To help in securing facilities or forms of protection needed in the community for better family living;

To try to determine the effect of certain laws or movements on the welfare of families;

To be concerned for the improvement of family life in this and other countries.

CHAPTER II

Effects of Technological, Scientific, and Educational Developments on Type of Program Offered and Needed

When one looks back over the period of less than one hundred years during which the schools have done any work in areas now thought of as home economics, it is clear that different needs have been recognized for the program, and that many technological, scientific, and educational developments have affected society, the home, and thus the kind of program required. All education for girls developed slowly in this country and home economics (at first called domestic economy) was originally advocated by those concerned for the education of girls. Only in the latter part of the eighteenth century (150 years after the beginning of education for boys) did schools begin gradually to admit girls—and then only for a few hours a day when boys were not in attendance. Equal provision for the education of girls was not generally made until well into the nineteenth century.[1]

Historical Development

During the early years of the nineteenth century, outstanding women pleaded for the education of girls. Mrs. Emma Hart Willard, who ran a private school for girls in Middlebury, Vermont, was one of these. In 1818, she urged the New York State Legislature to provide a state grant for girls' education comparable to that allotted to boys' education.

The influence of individuals and books. Another woman, Catherine Beecher (1800–78), who ran a private school in Hartford, Connecticut, from 1820 to 1832 (and, later, another in Cincinnati with her sister, Harriet Beecher Stowe), was also a leader in

---

[1] Thomas Woody, *A History of Women's Education* (New York: The Science Press, 1929), Vol. I, pp. 106, 144.

17

promoting the education of women. In 1841 her book, *A Treatise on Domestic Economy,* was published. The chapter titles—"Peculiar Responsibilities of American Women," "Healthful Food," "Clothing," "Cleanliness," "Domestic Manners," "Care of Infants," "Construction of Houses"—give some indication of the contents. This book and others Beecher wrote between 1869 and 1873 on *The American Woman's Home* and *Principles of Domestic Science* were helpful to teachers later.

Arguments presented.   In the preface to her first book, Miss Beecher wrote:

> The author of this work was led to attempt it by discovering, in her extensive travels, the deplorable sufferings of multitudes of young wives and mothers from the combined influence of poor health, poor domestics, and a defective education.
>
> The measure which, more than any other, would tend to remedy this evil would be to place domestic economy on an equality with the other sciences in female schools. This should be done because it can be properly and systematically taught (not practically, but as a science), as much so as political economy or moral science, or any other branch of study; because this science can never be properly taught until it is made a branch of learning; and because this method will secure a dignity and importance in the estimation of young girls which can never be accorded while they perceive their teachers and parents practically attaching more value to every other department of science than this.[2]

Kinds of courses offered.   Although the arguments for establishing the program dealt with improving the lot of women and improving living for the family, the descriptions sent to the U.S. Bureau of Education by state and city superintendents of schools were of courses in sewing and cooking and were often taught to girls while boys were taking courses in manual training.[3] Sewing was to a large extent the teaching of processes through the making of samples. According to Superintendent of Schools Powell of Washington, D.C.:

> This work has served a double purpose, that of giving instruction in sewing, and another, that of interest in other school work.[4]

---

[2] Benjamin R. Andrews, *Education for the Home,* Part I, U.S. Bureau of Education Bulletin No. 36 (Washington, D.C.: USGPO, 1914), p. 11.

[3] *Report of the Commissioner of Education for the Year 1887–88,* Chap. XV, "Manual and Industrial Training" (Washington, D.C.: USGPO, 1888).

[4] *Ibid.,* p. 861.

In teaching cooking or housekeeping, emphasis was given to the reasons underlying procedures—a result perhaps of the clarification by early scientists of the scientific principles involved. General Francis Walker, President of Massachusetts Institute of Technology, said of this new emphasis:

> We are not driven to defend the introduction of cooking into the public schools as an invasion of the proper field of education, justified by due necessity. No one can spend an hour in the cooking schools of Boston . . . without being impressed by the very high education value of the instruction given. As a great object lesson in chemistry; as a means of promoting care, patience, and forethought; as a study of cause and effect; as a medium of conveying useful information, irrespective altogether of the practical value of the art required, the short course which alone the means at command allowed to be given to each class of girls has constituted, I do not doubt, the best body of purely educational training which any girl of all those classes ever experienced within the same number of hours.[5]

Contributions of scientists.   Two men who helped to clarify the scientific principles taught in these courses were a physicist, Benjamin Thompson, known as Count Rumford (1753–1814), and a chemist, Edward Youmans (1821–87), who, in 1858, published a book called *Household Science*. Reports of their studies discussed the relation of these sciences to home use of fuels, cooking ranges, utensils, baking, the making of soup and coffee, lighting, and ventilation.

The person whose books and leadership have been most influential was another scientist, Mrs. Ellen H. Richards (1842–1911). Mrs. Richards was a graduate of Vassar and the first woman student to be admitted (1871) to the Massachusetts Institute of Technology, where she became a sanitary chemist and later a member of the faculty. Finding that teachers were being asked to teach science without having had much preparation, she helped to raise money to provide laboratory space for women in the Institute, conducted correspondence courses in science, and wrote several books. Her *Food Materials and their Adulteration,* published in 1885, was followed by *The Chemistry of Cooking and Cleaning, The Cost of Living, The Cost of Food, The Cost of Shelter, The Art of Right Living,* and *Euthenics.*

---

[5] *Ibid.,* p. 851.

The Lake Placid Conferences. Mrs. Richards and Mr. Melvil Dewey, Director of the State Library and Director of Home Education in New York State, organized the Lake Placid conferences (see also p. 1) to consider "some united action on the part of those most interested in home science or household economics." [6] Mrs. Richards served as chairman of the constantly growing group.

At the third conference, a committee presented an outline of a course of study which was to begin in the lower grades and, in the upper grades, to emphasize the reasons why certain procedures are followed. This course of study was to draw from principles of science and economics and emphasize a sense of responsibility in the home:

> In the high school the activities continue, but are perhaps less prominent; the scientific aspect is further emphasized, and the economics fully developed. The definite subjects of study are food, in its relation to nutrition; clothing, in its relation to health and as embodying the beautiful; the house with its artistic and hygienic furnishing, its sanitation and practical management; the health of the household as dependent on personal hygiene and including the care of little children, and of those who are ill and injured.[7]

Growth of the school and college programs. During the late 1800's and early 1900's, there was rapid growth in the number of schools teaching home economics. A survey made in 1913 of 444 cities indicated that twenty-seven of those cities had introduced instruction in some aspect of home economics by 1895 and ninety-one had introduced it by 1900.[8] In 1914, Andrews found home economics included in school programs in all the states and in "not less than 3500 or more towns and cities." [9]

At the college level, Iowa State University (formerly Iowa College of Agriculture and Mechanics Arts), Kansas State University (formerly Kansas Agricultural College), and The University of Illinois (formerly Illinois Industrial University) introduced home economics between 1872 and 1874. By 1890, the Iowa and Kansas institutions and five other higher institutions had organized four-

[6] Lake Placid Conferences on Home Economics, *Proceedings of the First Conference* (Lake Placid, N.Y., 1899), p. 4.

[7] Lake Placid Conference on Home Economics, *Proceedings of the Third Conference, supplement* (Lake Placid, N.Y., 1901), pp. 5–6.

[8] Benjamin R. Andrews, *Education for the Home,* Part II, U.S. Bureau of Education Bulletin No. 37 (Washington, D.C.: USGPO, 1915), pp. 69–70.

[9] *Ibid.,* p. 68.

year courses in the field.[10] By 1914, there were 252 colleges and universities reporting definite courses of instruction in household science and not less than 12,000 (in 1914–15) college students preparing for teaching household arts for homemaking or for household administration and dietetics.[11]

The influence of legislation, state and federal. Between 1905 and 1920, legislation played an important part in the development of the school program in home economics. By 1914, approximately three fourths of the states had authorized education for the home as a subject of instruction; thirty, as a subject for elementary schools; thirty-three, as a subject for secondary schools.[12] Eleven states were supplementing authorization by giving direct or indirect grants-in-aid to elementary schools for instruction in home economics. Twenty-nine states gave similar grants to secondary schools.[13] Most of this legislation involved also the promotion of manual training and agricultural and/or industrial education. This represents the beginning of vocational education.

While the state legislatures were passing laws to provide for such education within their borders, some national organizations and groups were urging support by the federal government. As early as 1907, a bill was introduced in the House and Senate to provide aid for instruction in agriculture, mechanic arts, and home economics.[14] In succeeding years, bills were introduced in the Congress in one form or another to provide federal aid for vocational education. Finally, in February, 1917, the Vocational Education (Smith-Hughes) Act was passed.[15]

The stimulus to home economics education provided by this national measure has had a marked influence on the program. The law made available to the states funds for agricultural, trade, home economics, and industrial education of less than college grade to

---

[10] Benjamin R. Andrews, *Education for the Home, Colleges, and Universities*, Part III, U.S. Bureau of Education Bulletin No. 38 (Washington, D.C.: USGPO, 1915), pp. 63–67.

[11] Andrews, *Education for the Home, Colleges, and Universities*, Part III, *Ibid.*, p. 82.

[12] Andrews, *Education for the Home*, Part II, *op. cit.*, pp. 7, 8.

[13] *Ibid.*, pp. 9, 10.

[14] Lloyd E. Blauch, *Federal Cooperation in Agricultural Extension Work, Vocational Education and Vocational Rehabilitation*, U.S. Department of Interior, Office of Education, Bulletin No. 15 (Washington, D.C.: USGPO, 1933), p. 53.

[15] *Ibid.*, Chaps. VI, VII.

pupils fourteen years of age and over in schools under public supervision and control, and for the preparation and professional improvement of teachers of these subjects. The funds could be used for reimbursement of salaries of teachers of these subjects in day, part-time, and evening schools, and were matched by state or local funds or both. The purpose, to train students for "useful employment," was interpreted, in home economics, to mean the preparation of girls and women for useful employment as daughters and homemakers.

Kind of program supported.   An analysis of the job of homemaking, made shortly after the federal law was passed, furnished a basis for the kind of program which could be financed by vocational education funds. Homemaking was defined as a social and business enterprise, the homemaker as a joint manager who is the purchasing agent, a partner in the business (and usually the business manager). As the superintendent of the plant, she plans her own work and that of others and must be skilled in general housekeeping, in the preparation and serving of food, in sewing (especially in the remaking and care and repair of clothing), in the care and rearing of children, and in the care of the family's health. She is the educational manager, the health and welfare manager, and the social manager of the family group.[16]

This analysis served to encourage the development of a program which differed from that associated with the manual training movement, but one consistent with that advocated at the Lake Placid Conferences. Local communities were responsible for providing facilities that would make it possible to teach this more comprehensive program.

Appropriations to the states through the George-Deen Law (1936) and the George-Barden Law (1946) made it possible for home economics teachers to encourage pupil experiences in the home and in the community as well as in the school and helped to provide conference periods for the teacher so she could visit pupils' homes and better guide the experiences of the individual pupil.

The purpose of home economics in the vocational program has been focused on the home throughout the years: The different way of stating it is a recognition of charging home situations. In 1919

[16] *Home Economics Education and Organization,* Federal Board for Vocational Education Bulletin No. 28 (Washington, D.C.: USGPO, 1922), pp. 15, 16.

it was "to reach all groups of girls and women with a type of home-making training which will function immediately in the solution of daily problems of homemaking." [17] In 1958, the objective was broadened: to provide "instruction which will enable families to improve the quality of their family life through more effective de-velopment and utilization of human and material resources." [18]

Some people have been under the impression that home econom-ics was introduced into the schools for the purpose of preparing servants for employment in homes of others rather than for devel-oping in daughters of school board members and other citizens the ability to manage their own homes effectively. A careful study of the records provides no justification for this viewpoint. The argu-ments for home economics—both those advanced in the late nine-teenth century and those advanced in the first decades of the twentieth century (including the arguments for vocational educa-tion in home economics)—have indicated that the fundamental purpose of this type of education was the preparation of students for homemaking and family living. This is sound thinking from many standpoints: homes have a profound influence on the quality of individuals (including the kind of workmen and professional people they become); preparation for homemaking is as vital to society as preparation for any occupation outside the home; and carrying on the work of the home—managing the money and other family resources—makes as great a contribution to the general eco-nomic welfare as does money earned through outside employment.

Some results of vocational education upon the home economics program. Two features of the vocational program have helped to strengthen home economics in the secondary schools: the focus on preparation for homemaking; and the availability of funds to assist in preparing home economics teachers and in encouraging schools to offer a broader program. Through this encouragement, schools have come to include education in more aspects of family living. The relative narrowness of the earlier program was revealed in the study made by Andrews in 1913–14 in 288 high schools. Eighty-nine per cent of these schools offered courses in some phases of

---

[17] Federal Board for Vocational Education, *Annual Report to Congress* (Wash-ington, D.C.: USGPO, 1919), p. 44.

[18] *Administration of Vocational Education,* Vocational Education Bulletin No. 1 (Washington, D.C.: USGPO, 1958), p. 15.

food and nutrition; 81 per cent offered courses in sewing, textiles, or costume design; but only 25 per cent provided courses in some phase of shelter, housekeeping, or management.[19] Other aspects were neglected.

Another proof of the need for change in the program was given in 1922 by the Commission on Home Economics, appointed by the Commission on the Reorganization of Secondary Education of The National Education Association:

> Heretofore the aims have been too narrow and the content too limited. . . . The methods have been too didactic. . . . Teaching . . . has not been adequately articulated with home life and home experiences. Its [general home economics] development has been affected by many forces: Unwise economy has dictated the use of small quantities of material; large classes have necessitated uniform progress by all pupils; the employment of inexperienced and young teachers has resulted in methods imitating those used by academic teachers; the employment of untrained teachers has led the directors to provide uniform and rigid courses; long hours of teaching have prohibited the establishment of contacts with the homes of the school community.[20]

Many of these difficulties have been overcome since 1922, though some aspects of home economics still receive too little attention and there is overemphasis on the development of manual skills[21]—a carryover, perhaps, from the manual training movement.

Kinds of growth stimulated. A few figures compiled from state reports and summarized in annual reports to Congress by the Federal Board for Vocational Education illustrate some of the developments resulting from federal encouragement. The enrollment of pupils increased rapidly in day school programs of home economics which met state vocational requirements (from 8439 in 1918 to 12,445 in 1919, 30,936 in 1923, and 44,261 in 1927).[22] In 1961 the day school enrollment in home economics in vocational programs was 958,496 girls and 22,613 boys.

---

[19] Andrews, *Education for the Home,* Part II, *op. cit.,* p. 106.

[20] *Reorganization of Home Economics in Secondary Schools,* Department of Interior, Bureau of Education Bulletin No. 5 (Washington, D.C.: USGPO, 1922), p. 3.

[21] Beulah I. Coon, *Home Economics in the Public Secondary Schools,* U.S. Department of Health, Education and Welfare, Office of Education Circular No. 661 (Washington, D.C.: USGPO, 1962), Chap. VII.

[22] Federal Board for Vocational Education, *Annual Report to Congress* (Washington, D.C.: USGPO, 1927), p. 35.

Six states had supervisors of home economics in 1917. By 1919 ten states had full-time supervisors, and thirty-four had part-time supervisors. At first, supervisors were hired without specific standards for their qualifications. By 1919, the standard required completion of a four-year college program planned for the preparation of teachers, two to four years' successful teaching experience and two or three years' experience in homemaking.[23]

Before 1917, the required preparation for teachers of home economics varied from a summer's work to four years of college. In 1917 many home economics teachers had had only two years of preparation. By 1919 the Annual Report stated: "the length of the teacher-training course as now outlined is four years in all but four States and two are now developing a four-year course." By 1924, no state accepted teachers in all-day schools with vocational programs in home economics who had had less than four years of college preparation.[24]

Changes in the home economics program in the public schools necessitated changes in the teacher education program. It was essential that those in charge of home economics education have preparation in home economics subject matter and in education, for they were responsible for teaching home economics methods courses and for directing student teaching. There was need, too, to broaden the teacher preparation curriculum to include courses and experience in home management, child development, and family-community relationships. For example, in 1917 there were no organized courses of instruction in child care in teacher preparation institutions; in 1922 such courses were offered in twenty-five institutions.[25]

A plan for in-service education of supervisors and teacher educators was initiated by home economics staff members of The Federal Board for Vocational Education in 1918. Annual conferences for this purpose were held until the 1950's; since then they have been held every other year. At these conferences, common problems were discussed, study groups were formed to work on specific questions, and committees were organized to deal with matters of importance to state programs. Similarly, most state supervisors and

---

[23] Federal Board for Vocational Education, *Annual Report to Congress* (Washington, D.C.: USGPO, 1925), p. 53.

[24] *Ibid.*, p. 55.

[25] *Ibid.*, p. 58.

teacher educators have held annual conferences for home economics teachers to work on teaching problems.

This historical sketch indicates some of the forces which have shaped the home economics program in the secondary schools from its beginnings as a part of the manual training movement through its development, in the Lake Placid Conferences and in the early years of vocational education. Its close relation to science and economics was stressed in the late nineteenth century, and its relation to other social sciences, psychology, and art has been emphasized throughout this century. The purpose of home economics—the strengthening of family life—has been basic in the thinking of all the leaders in the field.

School Changes

In tracing the historical development of home economics, those influences directly affecting the program have been touched upon. There were many other factors in the first half of the twentieth century which affected the total school program and, thus, home economics. Among these influences are the junior high school movement, which brought a somewhat different focus into programs for Grades 7, 8, and 9; the consolidation of small schools into larger school units, making possible the teaching of a wider variety of subjects in one secondary school; and the marked increase in the proportion of young people attending high school, resulting in a more heterogeneous group and permitting the development of programs to meet a greater variety of needs. The last few years have made available to schools the use of radio, recordings, educational television, and teaching machines, creating a wider variety of teaching techniques for which teachers need to be prepared. The increase in research in education and psychology provides a sounder base for understanding youth and for developing effective methods of teaching. Schools are experimenting with much less rigid techniques, with different groupings of pupils and different sizes of classes, and with the use of laymen to assume some of the responsibilities teachers have carried. All these developments are important to home economics teachers, as they are to other teachers, and are affecting the programs offered.

Types of Changes Affecting
Homes and Home Economics

These educational developments—the manual training movement, the vocational movement, the changes in school organization and personnel, the increased research and experiments on school problems—are only part of the picture of change which has importance for the program in home economics. Social, economic, scientific, and technological changes which have had and are having a tremendous influence on the home have been occurring at a quickening speed. As these changes occur, a revamping of the program which home economics offers is essential. Modern living demands that the gap which has existed between what is happening to society and what the school does to prepare future members of that society should be closed as tightly as possible. Tyler states this well:

> . . . the time lag between major changes and our adaptation to these changes has become a much more serious threat to our development and even to our survival than ever before in history.[26]

Since it is impossible to predict future changes, teachers in every area must be constantly alert and they must continuously ask what the changes which are occurring portend for the school program.

A brief summary of some of the changes was given by James Montgomery, at the fiftieth anniversary meeting of The American Home Economics Association:

> The changes that have pounded the social, economic, and technological shores of our land over the past fifty years have been precipitous and all-encompassing. We have emerged from a predominantly rural nation of some 92 million people to an urban nation of 175 million people; from extreme physical and social isolation to a state of being in which we are seldom out of sight or sound of mass media; from a time when the place of women was in the home to a time when their place is in the home, the office, and the factory; from a concern for high infant mortality rates to a concern for rediscovering the potentials of the aged; and from a time when *laissez faire* was the ruler of the land to a time when the triad of big business, big government, and big unions holds sway over us all.[27]

[26] Ralph W. Tyler, "Education in a World of Change," *Journal of Home Economics,* Vol. 54, No. 7 (September, 1962), 527–28.

[27] James Montgomery, "Current Developments and a Look Ahead in Housing and Household Equipment," *Journal of Home Economics,* Vol. 51, No. 7 (September, 1959), 581.

A program concerned with the home and with family life cannot ignore such all-encompassing changes. The accelerating rate of change demands a continuous evolution. It is apparent that a program adapted to the early part of the century will not satisfy the needs of the second half of the century. In fact, a program adapted to the early 1940's is not adapted to the early 1960's. A few changes are indicated and some of their meaning for home economics is briefly discussed.

Rural to urban to suburban living.   In 1910 about one in three persons lived on a farm. The family was a relatively independent production unit. In 1960, however, only one of ten persons lived on a farm. The United States has become primarily an industrial economy; the home is now primarily a consumption unit. Between 1910 and 1920, about one sixth of the growth of the population was in suburban areas; between 1940 and 1950 these areas accounted for one half of the growth. Both the city and the suburb have brought family members into closer proximity to others and given them a wider diversity of contacts.

With suburban living has come more home ownership and more space and family freedom, but not the relative independence of farm life. For many families, houses have been too small to give satisfaction; the houses are often identical to or very nearly like those of the neighbors; many are shoddy and unattractive and are adequate for no more than the immediate family. Many suburban communities lack trees and recreational facilities; others have expensive or inadequate utilities, roads, education, and other public services. Many husbands have to commute and many young wives and mothers, without relatives near, are more alone than they have ever been. Suburbs have also separated the middle and upper classes from minority and low-income groups and from less well-educated families, possibly giving rise to a lack of the understanding among groups so important to a democratic society. The use of mechanized equipment has replaced much of the physical effort formerly required of the homemaker, her relative, or the domestic servant (who is now seldom available).

These changes have brought to families new types of problems which the home economics program should recognize. Although many of the manual skills that were formerly needed in the home no longer need be emphasized, the home economics program must now prepare pupils for the decisions involved in buying and using mechanized equipment; in buying and preparing canned, frozen, or precooked packaged foods, the nutritive value of which is difficult to determine; in selecting ready-to-wear clothing, which often accounts for ninety cents of every dollar spent by the family for clothes; and in choosing among commercial laundering, drycleaning, and many other kinds of services. Preparation should include the new types of relationships which have developed as a result of smaller living space and isolation of generations and cultural groups. Community resources must be assessed and individuals prepared to make use of them if adequate public services and acceptable essential commercial services are available to families. These types of problems in management, consumer education, and family, personal, and family-community relations replace most of those of former days.

Increasing population.   Other types of population changes have brought different problems to families and to communities. The population explosion after World War II (from 152 million in 1950 to 188 million in 1962 and a predicted 235 million by 1975) has created a need for more and bigger houses as well as for more educational facilities and teachers, and has given rise to concern lest the educational needs of young people cannot be met.

Improved health conditions have resulted in an increasing proportion of the population in the upper age group. In 1960, 16 million people in the United States were sixty-five years of age or older. This group is expected to increase to 25 million by 1980. Although most of the older citizens have some income, some 50–60 per cent of them

> have incomes of less than $1000 per year. About half have assets of less than $1000. The most common asset of greater value is a home. Medical costs for those over sixty-five will be approximately twice that for the average member of the total population.[28]

The increased proportion of aging citizens in the population raises the question as to how those with so little income are to be cared for and how their needs in nutrition, housing, health, medical care, recreation, and social relations will best be met.

---

[28] *The Nation and its Older People,* Report of the White House Conference on Aging, January 9–12, 1961 (Washington, D.C.: USGPO, 1961), p. 117.

The increased numbers of children complicate the life of many young mothers, especially with their husbands away for long days and their relatives usually living in another community. Developing managerial ability and understanding and skill in child development is therefore more important than ever.

Occupation changes.   The changes in occupations have not been confined to those from farming to industry, though 20 per cent of the total number of farm workers, or 1.6 million, left the farm from 1950 to 1960.[29] Automation is rapidly taking over the unskilled, routine, and semiskilled jobs, requiring that more and more people develop technical, professional, or managerial skills. Thus the period of education is necessarily lengthened. Although more people were employed in production than in service industries until late in the 1940's, there were in 1960 "over 25 per cent more employees in service than in production industries, with an increase of over five million in less than ten years." [30]

Not only is more education demanded, but it is increasingly necessary to expect education and re-education to be continued throughout life. Deciding upon the kind of education for young people is more difficult with so many uncertainties about the future. More long-range planning for meeting the rising costs of education is needed. Fear of job insecurity affects many families. All of these are relatively new aspects of management, family economics, and family relations with which many families need help. In addition, home economists must face the question of whether there are service occupations or technical skills which require understanding and abilities which they are best prepared to develop and should make available through the schools (see p. 44).

The employment of women.   In 1960, 3.66 million more women were working outside the home than was the case in 1945. One third of all women workers have children under eighteen years of age and 2.5 million have children under six. What type of care is being given these small children? What does a mother's employment mean for the teen-ager? Nine out of ten women work for at least part of their lives. Many enter the labor market after they are

---

[29] *Goals for Americans,* A Report of the President's Commission on National Goals (Englewood Cliffs, N.J.: Prentice-Hall, Inc., 1960), p. 197.
[30] *Ibid.,* p. 197.

fifty. Are women being adequately educated both for homemaking and for outside responsibilities? [31]

Since more women are working, many men are helping by carrying some of the home responsibilities: caring for the children, shopping, preparing food, and caring for the house. Men are no more likely to be able to carry these responsibilities wisely without preparation than are women. Provision for education in child development, family relations, nutrition, food preparation, and consumer education is now an important consideration for young men as well as for young women.

Mass communication and transportation. The extent and speed of mass communication and transportation have changed the lives of young and old. Radio, television, and jet planes are bringing contacts and news from all parts of the world. Besides the effects which these changes are having on young children and teen-agers— changes with which homemakers must cope—the individual and the family now have more responsibility for what is happening to families in other parts of the country and the world. "Man lives in ever closer proximity to his fellow man." He can know and see, instantly or within a few hours, what is happening in any part of the world. Each individual must be concerned about those living in poverty, those racked by disease or by hunger, and those with little or no education and no chance for education.

New research and new products. For almost every job of the homemaker new products, equipment, or tools are being developed. The homemaker must learn to become a wise consumer of processed foods, automatic equipment, and new fibers and fabrics. What are the merits and disadvantages of some twenty different fibers, many of which have been developed only within the last few years? How will blends of different fibers perform in clothing or in home furnishings? Which vacuum cleaner has the qualities needed by a given household? On what bases can one choose among the 6000 or more products in the supermarket? How does a given choice affect the market situation? What local merchandising regulations are being observed and what new ones needed in the community?

---

[31] Mildred Weigley Wood, Alberta Hill, and Edna P. Amidon, *Management Problems of Homemakers Employed Outside the Home,* U.S. Department of Health, Education and Welfare, Office of Education OE-83009 (Washington, D.C.: USGPO, 1961).

The homemaker of the 1960's needs to be familiar not only with the research resulting in new products and services but also with the research affecting the health and welfare of family members. What are the latest findings on fats, amino acids, and minerals which one should know to provide healthful meals for family members? What is the soundest research on child growth and development which she and her husband should be aware of in guiding children wisely? What is the effect of new methods of preservation and packaging on the nutritive values of foods?

The Meaning for Home Economics

What happens in the community, the nation, and the world has its impact on the family. By the same token, the way families react affects what happens in the community, the nation, and the world. In developing her pupils' ability to think, to solve problems, and to become more sensitive to factors affecting homes, the home economics teacher must be continuously reappraising what is important to families. Many of the changes which are occurring have highlighted the significance in home economics of family relationships, child development, consumer education, family economics, and management.

Patterns of personal and social relationships are often indelibly determined by the relationships which exist within the family. Are young people being given the kind of help needed in developing satisfying relationships with their peers, with their parents, and with different age and cultural groups? Are they gaining enough understanding of children and their development to give some wise guidance when they themselves become parents? Are they gaining a better understanding of themselves and of their emotions? Are they developing the ability to adjust to new environments, to the diversity of brief contacts which modern living requires?

The infinite number of decisions which adults have to make for the family in the selection and purchase of goods and services are presented to youth in somewhat modified form. The amount and kind of advertising directed at teen-agers makes it imperative that they be able to evaluate it objectively if they are to become wise consumers.

Many decisions have to be made by the individual family, but the growing interdependence of families makes it essential that family members learn to evaluate what should be done by the individual family and what can better be done cooperatively with other individuals and groups. For example, what can be done by producers and consumers working together to determine what is needed by families? What kinds of labels are needed on clothing, textiles, foods, equipment, and furnishings to serve as a guide to the buyer? How can these be made available? What joint undertakings will make for better radio or television programs? for a safe and adequate water supply? for improved educational facilities and personnel? for better facilities for the care of children? for the care of the aged? What regulations or laws are needed to protect the wholesomeness of food or the quality and the price of drugs? The management decisions made by the family often make the difference between health and disease, between having excellent goods or shoddy products on the market. And these decisions often make it possible for the family to attain its own values and goals while helping others attain theirs. To make these decisions wisely calls for knowledge and for an understanding of the wider implications of decisions made.

Many of the goals of a school program in home economics at the beginning of the century are still valid. But the changed circumstances in which families live has made the kind of home economics useful then as outdated as the kind of physics which was adequate before the atomic age. Families, frequently mobile, whether living in cities, suburbs, or rural areas demand a background for decision-making not required in the relative isolation of the rural economy of the early 1900's. This becomes more necessary with many wives and mothers working outside the home, with new types of contacts for all family members, with mass media of communication reaching every individual, with new products to be evaluated, new research to be mastered, and with new problems arising day by day. A program incorporating new types of consumption, human relationships, and management problems within the community, as well as the national and international implications, is essential in the second half of the twentieth century.

CHAPTER III

Planning for Junior and Senior
High School Pupils

Home economics, as a separate subject of instruction, appears first in most school systems in Grades 7, 8, or 9. A very few schools offer it earlier than the seventh grade. In 1959, a nationwide sampling of junior high schools revealed that 63 per cent of the seventh-grade girls and 73 per cent of the eighth-grade girls were enrolled in home economics.[1] In the earlier grades, there is likely to be some study of the family and of agencies or groups in the community that serve the family. Also, happy experiences in the home will have provided some pupils with satisfying social and family relations, pleasing environment, and interest in performing certain household tasks and in maintaining health and safety. These pupils will be ready to receive much basic information and to discover principles which will give them more independence in their home activities and decisions. Other pupils may have had almost no opportunity to share happily and efficiently in home life, and some may have developed attitudes and habits inconsistent with constructive family living. These pupils will need a different kind of help.

Recognizing Individual Differences

In almost any junior or senior high school class there will be wide differences in mental, physical, social, and emotional development. Mental age may vary much more widely than chronological age.[2] Many aspects of health, energy, posture, and physical development will be of concern to the home economics teacher. Achievement in

---

[1] Beulah I. Coon, *Home Economics in the Public Secondary Schools,* U.S. Department of Health, Education and Welfare, Office of Education Circular No. 661 (Washington, D.C.: USGPO, 1962), p. 32.

[2] Percival M. Symonds, *What Education Has to Learn from Psychology* (New York: Teachers College, Bureau of Publications, Columbia University, 1959), pp. 91–103.

various areas, including reading ability, will make a difference in what can be accomplished by different pupils. Capacity for achievement will vary among pupils, as will the stages reached in the maturing process. Each of these will influence what can be done in home economics classes.

There are many ways of coming to understand the individual differences which exist in a class. School records and cumulative records provide data on physical health and school achievement; anecdotal records assist in indicating possible approaches to adopt with different pupils. But one of the most important sources of information for home economics teachers is a visit to the home.[3] Some teachers make it a practice to visit the homes of prospective pupils who are to enroll in home economics for the first time. Such visits are very helpful in revealing the kinds of attitudes and abilities fostered in the home, and enable the teacher to set more realistic goals with pupils and to plan the kind of school and home experiences which will be most useful to them. Observation may reveal many basic differences among pupils which will suggest needs for later study. Some pretests are also useful for discovering pupils' understandings, skills, and attitudes which may be built upon or which need to be developed. Taking time to plan with pupils for those goals which are important is valuable to the teacher and promotes a sense of responsibility for achievement in the pupil.

Junior High School Pupils

Whether the school is organized as an eight-year elementary school followed by a four-year high school, or as a six-year elementary school followed by a junior and senior high school, most of the seventh-, eighth-, and ninth-grade pupils, though manifesting many individual differences, will be in the preadolescent and early adolescent stages of development.

Early adolescent concerns. Prescott has listed the following as the developmental tasks faced by the early adolescent girl in our society:

[3] Drusilla Kent, *et al., Home, School, and Community Experiences in the Home-making Program,* U.S. Department of Health, Education and Welfare, Vocational Division Bulletin, No. 252 (Washington, D.C.: USGPO, 1957), 60–61; and Daniel A. Prescott, *The Child in the Educative Process* (New York: McGraw-Hill Book Company, Inc., 1957), pp. 161–67.

1. Learning the significance of the physical changes occurring as a result of growth, especially of the maturing of her reproductive capacity, and learning how to maintain health at the new maturity level.

2. Learning ways of grooming, dressing, and behaving that are appropriate to her sex and effective in attracting favorable attention from boys, other girls, and adults.

3. Learning how to get along well with boys in the light of her new body dynamics and maturity level.

4. Learning how to get along well with girls in the light of her new heterosexual roles and maturity level.

5. Winning and effectively playing adolescent peer-group roles in the school and community.

6. Winning from parents the right to make decisions and to be responsible for a wider range of her own behavior.

7. Maintaining security-giving love relationships with her parents despite her striving for greater freedom to make decisions for herself.

8. Continuing her successful accomplishment of school tasks and winning adult approval in and about school.

9. Learning about and participating in social institutions and processes, and learning her duties and responsibilities as a citizen.

10. Exploring possible adult roles such as homemaking, caring for children, taking part in community affairs, and choosing a vocation.

11. Exploring questions about the meaning of life and about the values to be sought in life.

12. Continuing the development of a code of ethics as a measuring stick for evaluating her own attitudes and her actual behavior.

13. Setting up goals for immediate accomplishment as a step toward long-term purposes.[4]

Though boys usually mature somewhat later, most of these tasks apply equally to boys in the early stages of adolescence. Individual pupils will be working at these tasks at different rates. Each will be attempting to understand and to assimilate the changes taking place. The varied patterns of development of members of the peer group make the task more difficult and the teacher will be watching for those factors which influence the rate of physical, emotional, and social maturation; for variations in achievement and in capacity for achievement; for interest in following a rigid program or a desire for creativity, initiative, independence; for those pupils who have a realistic perception of themselves and those who are confused, self-conscious, shy, or overly aggressive. She will be aware that few will be able to maintain a completely stable, consistent

---

4 Prescott, *op. cit.*, pp. 279–80.

attitude. She may find some lacking in the security of an affectionate family life, and others trying to loosen family bonds and establish new relations with family and friends.

Home economics for seventh- and eighth-grade pupils. The rapid changes in physical growth, in social and emotional reactions, and the need to rate with the peer group as well as with the family are factors which influence the kind of home economics program needed. Many girls, exploring possible adult roles, are especially interested in young children; others may be interested in earning money by babysitting. To them, help in gaining some understanding of the interests and abilities of children at different ages and knowledge of ways to give wise guidance will be helpful and, at the same time, will serve as an aid in gaining some further understanding of themselves.[5] If they are earning money and/or have an allowance, a study of where their money goes, whether they are getting what they really want with it, and how they can plan for greater satisfaction is important. Specific help in how to buy for themselves and their families is pertinent.

The tasks of early adolescents indicate that most are ready to profit by a study of friendships and of ways to plan and carry through simple forms of hospitality. Their growing interest in personal appearance provides a basis for help in grooming and care of clothing and a study of ways in which food habits and nutrition may contribute to their personal attractiveness. They will enjoy preparing nutritious snacks and very simple meals, and planning for these as a part of a well-chosen diet. Some skill in the care of clothing and the house and in the preparation of food is of interest to many, and these skills often serve to win approval from other members of the family. Detailed help is usually needed in establishing efficient and sanitary work habits, so that time and energy may be saved in the more routine activities.

As pupils pursue some of these interests, they should be assisted in drawing generalizations in the different areas to serve as guides for their later actions and decisions. The generalizations will be likely to include the results of good nutrition, the efficient arrangement of supplies and equipment, time- and energy-saving procedures,

[5] Lucy McCormack, "Child Development Observation in a Secondary School Program," *Journal of Home Economics,* Vol. 51, No. 2 (February, 1959), 100–101.

play activities and toys suitable for children of various ages, ways to care for different types of clothing so as to maintain an attractive personal appearance, guides for making a room more attractive and for sharing in its care, and the place of youth in carrying family responsibilities.

The amount of time spent on home economics varies with the school. Many schools offer a one-year program, with classes meeting five times a week in seventh and/or eighth grades (often one semester each year). This makes it possible to take advantage of the changing concerns of rapidly growing pupils. If the time available does not permit scheduling five classes a week for a semester, a blocked plan with other subjects for nine, ten, or twelve weeks usually results in a greater feeling of accomplishment than one or two classes a week, which was an early pattern.

Home economics for ninth-grade pupils. In the ninth grade, the home economics program is usually offered daily for the full year and provides an opportunity for pupils to study several aspects of home economics of interest to them as participating, responsible family members. Real progress will have been made by some in achieving some of the developmental tasks of early adolescence; others will still need help with a large number of these tasks. Many ninth-grade pupils can sustain interest over a somewhat longer period than pupils in the seventh and eighth grades, so projects at this level can be more comprehensive. Also, their muscular coordination is usually better than that of children in the seventh and eighth grades. Pupils continue to be interested in understanding themselves and their reactions; many carry more responsibilities at home; most are still trying to gain independence from the family while maintaining security within it. They often need guidance in establishing their identity with both sex groups and in setting standards for relations with the opposite sex. They need to feel like others in the peer group, to gain success with them, and to accept differences in themselves and in others. In this grade it is possible to expect most pupils to be more precise in stating generalizations. To make this discussion more concrete, an illustration is given of the way in which the program in the three grades is sometimes organized. The topics suggest the particular aspects within which adaptations can be made for individual differences.

Seventh- and eighth-grade emphasis

1. Living happily with family and friends: making and keeping friends; having fun with family and friends.

2. Playing with and caring for children and helping to guide their learning.

3. Selecting and preparing foods for health—including buying, storing, preparing, and serving nutritious snacks or a simple meal—and caring for the kitchen.

4. Taking care of clothing: choosing and buying some articles of clothing; taking daily and weekly care of clothes; making a simple garment.

5. Helping at home: caring for bedroom; planning and spending own money; helping with family shopping; assisting with housekeeping.

Ninth-grade emphasis

1. Understanding self and others: understanding personal development; understanding parents and other adults; developing boy-girl relations.

2. Sharing family responsibilities: managing own money and planning with family for use of time and money; entertaining friends.

3. Understanding some needs and reactions of children of different ages.

4. Preparing food for the family: planning for nutrition; buying and storing food; preparing and serving simple meals; managing for wise use of time and money.

5. Planning personal wardrobe: buying clothes; making a simple garment.

6. Adding to the attractiveness of the home and sharing in family celebrations; making home more safe.

In some four-year high schools whose students come from a number of elementary schools, there will often be ninth-grade pupils who have had no home economics in seventh and eighth grades while others will have had the equivalent of a full year. Providing for individual differences becomes more complex than usual under these conditions. This can, however, usually be managed by developing these areas—but with more emphasis for those pupils who have had no home economics on the aspects suggested for the seventh and eighth grades. In communities where pupils are marrying young, the emphasis on boy-girl relations may need to be expanded to help pupils gain a greater understanding of these problems and to help them set standards for their conduct. For those pupils who are beginning to think of the vocations they hope to follow, some attention may well be given to the possibilities in home economics professions for those going on to college, and to related wage-earning opportunities for others. This problem may be covered in addition to, or as a substitute for, one of the units listed.

Senior High School Pupils

The amount and kind of home economics offered in the upper three grades of the secondary school differs with the size of the school and with the types of pupils enrolled. Besides the difference in amount of previous home economics, varying from none to two years, there will be other variations to consider. Some students will be interested in preparing for college; others will want to drop out of school. There will be gifted pupils and slow learners, and pupils from a wide variety of cultural backgrounds. In some schools a one-, two-, or three-year sequence is offered, often as a vocational program in homemaking. In some, a semester or a year's course, often called "Family Living," is offered for eleventh- or twelfth-grade pupils—both for those who have studied home economics and for those who have not. Some states, and some schools within a state, require one year of home economics of all girls; some, of all pupils. Usually home economics is offered as an elective course after the eighth grade.[6] In large high schools there are often special-interest home economics courses offered as electives.

Some adolescent concerns. As pupils become more mature, they are better able to accept their physique and their sex role and are more concerned with their new relations with the opposite sex. They are eager to develop adult patterns of social behavior and to become more economically and emotionally independent. Slowly they become aware of community and national issues. The home economics program can assist students in understanding themselves, in establishing more satisfying social and family relations, in considering what makes for happy marriages, in developing some managerial and consumer competences, in maintaining health and nutrition status, and in making homes attractive and adapting them to needs of family members. Through such study they should be helped to understand and use basic principles, to think more critically and creatively, and to be more sure of the values they feel are important.

[6] Coon, *op. cit.*, pp. 15–16.

Home economics for grades ten to twelve. In a national sampling study, 60 per cent of the ninth-grade girls were found to be enrolled in home economics; 40 per cent of the tenth-graders, 28 per cent of the eleventh-graders, and 34 per cent of the twelfth-graders. Enrollment of boys varied: 2 per cent in seventh and eighth grades, less than 1 per cent in ninth, tenth, and eleventh grades, and 3 per cent in twelfth grade.[7] Many of the tenth- and eleventh-grade courses are part of a sequence which begins in the ninth grade and more of them are offered as part of a vocational program than as nonvocational courses. Although the courses in all three grades were more frequently called "Home Economics" or "Homemaking," the title most frequently used in twelfth grade was "Family Living." [8]

Sequence of offerings (vocational). When a two-, three-, or (occasionally) four-year sequence beginning with the ninth grade is offered, it is usually focused on preparation for home and family living and is often presented as a vocational homemaking program. Enrollees may include girls who carry heavy responsibilities at home, those who plan to marry soon after high school, and those who, though they plan to go on to college, do not plan to take home economics there and want this more inclusive preparation for their home responsibilities.

This more intensive program usually provides greater opportunity for understanding the principles underlying social and family relations; selection, equipment, and care of houses and furnishings; care and development of infants and children; planning, preparation, and serving of meals to satisfy nutritional needs; buying, preserving, and storing of food; selection of textiles and selection, construction, and care of clothing; family economics and consumer education; management of resources to achieve goals and values for the individual, the family, and the community.

One year offerings in family living. Many schools are offering, for boys and girls in eleventh or twelfth grades, a one-year course (usually called "Family Living") which deals directly with many of their present and future family problems. Sometimes the course is designed for only a semester. The home economics teacher may

---

[7] *Ibid.,* pp. 32–37.
[8] *Ibid.,* p. 74.

teach it by herself, or she may share the teaching load with another teacher or with a guidance counselor. Some schools offer this course primarily for those pupils going on to college who will be likely to have little or no opportunity to study these problems before going into homes of their own. Other schools plan the course both for prospective college students and for those planning to enter the business world after high school.

In some situations, this course deals primarily with boy-girl relations, dating, marriage, family, social and community relations, and child development. Sometimes one semester is devoted to these problems and the second semester is devoted to family economics, consumer education, and management of resources. One or the other of these two plans is likely to be most useful because relationships, child development, and management are so important in modern family living. With some groups, however, it may be important to include—or to offer a separate course in—the selection and costs of housing, furnishings, equipment, food, and clothing, and to devote some attention to nutrition, meal management, and wardrobe planning. The greater maturity of twelfth-grade pupils and their wider background in science, social science, and art make it possible for them to find an intellectually challenging experience in the development of important concepts and principles which can be used in present family living and later in homes of their own.

Special interest courses. In the larger, comprehensive high schools it is often important to offer courses which are significant to special groups. These may be general courses or courses which concentrate on one phase of home economics.

In Philadelphia, where no new high school has been built since 1950 without a child development laboratory, child development is one of the most popular courses. In one new high school with an enrollment of 3000 boys and girls, 250 chose to enroll in child development in 1962, and 85 in home economics for the college-bound. In this city, there are four different possibilities for pupils who want to take home economics in Grades 10 to 12: (1) a full year of home economics can be taken as a fifth course (major) by choosing an academic curriculum. This course includes personal and family living, child care and development, home nursing, clothing, foods, housing, home furnishing, home management; (2) a girl may choose a college preparatory home economics curriculum which includes one five-periods-a-week course in home economics for each of three years; (3) a three-year homemaking curriculum meeting from six to ten periods a week is available—this may be a vocational home-making program; (4) a series of two-periods-a-week minors are offered in a wide variety of choices—home management, home care of the sick, housing and interior decoration, food and nutrition, personal and family living, in addition to child development.[9]

This variety of offerings meets the needs and interests of many types of pupils. In deciding on a program, one factor which may be useful is information on the mental ability of pupils. No widespread study of home economics pupils has been made, but in one Midwestern state, records of 1618 June, 1957, girl graduates in forty-six public high schools were analyzed for those who had enrolled in home economics and those who had not. "Almost two thirds of all enrollees were in the upper half of the IQ distribution." [10] In another state, of 316 ninth- and tenth-grade home economics pupils, in nineteen schools whose home economics programs had been judged by supervisors to be successful, fifty-eight had an IQ of 58–89; 203, of 90–110; and fifty-five of 111–148.[11]

Certain schools provide special courses or special emphasis within courses for some pupils in order to develop wage-earning skills related to homemaking as, for example, in food service and household occupations, or as assistants in child care centers, nurse's aids, and family aids in homes of the aged or others.

Other bases can be used for special interest courses. For scientifically inclined students, a study of the science of nutrition, food preparation, textiles, and equipment is of interest. Artistically gifted students find a challenge in the design of clothing and textiles and in the planning and furnishing of the home. The field of child development and family relations is of special interest to those concerned with social-psychological situations. (See also p. 779.)

In some schools it may be important to offer special work for the slow learners or for those who have reading difficulties. Their slower

---

[9] Supplied by Esther Hill, Director of Home Economics, School District of Philadelphia, in letter to author, November, 1962.

[10] Evelyn Irene Rouner, "A Contemporary Image of Home Economics Enrollees of Forty-Six Downstate Illinois Public High Schools," *Journal of Home Economics,* Vol. 54, No. 3 (March, 1962), 227.

[11] Jane Bemis, "Home Experiences of Ninth and Tenth Grade Pupils of Varying Abilities," *Journal of Home Economics,* Vol. 152, No. 3 (March, 1960), 208–209.

speed, their slower mental and motor development, their lower ability to generalize, and their need for practice and for a feeling of success can be met through the development of good food habits, good grooming, and some ability to assist in preparing family meals, caring for the house, choosing and wearing suitable clothing, mending and making simple garments, keeping accounts of expenditures and buying more wisely, caring for children, and maintaining satisfying relations with family and friends.

This brief sketch of ways in which home economics is being organized for secondary school pupils leaves out of consideration three closely related problems. Home economics in the thirteenth and fourteenth years, offered in technical institutes, community colleges, or junior colleges, may be a responsibility of the secondary school teacher. Also, about 40 per cent of the secondary schools have an adult education program in home economics which may consist of regularly scheduled classes or less formal methods of instruction. Finally, in some localities secondary school home economics teachers must serve as consultants to elementary school teachers and, on occasion, teach classes of elementary school pupils.

The development of youth during the adolescent period is tied closely to their relations with the family and their desire to achieve economic and social independence. The emphasis in home economics in junior and in senior high schools, therefore, is closely associated with this maturing process. The home economics program may help the early adolescent gain some understanding of himself and of others, some competence in certain home activities, and a better basis for making decisions about personal and family problems. Those in middle adolescence can be helped to become more competent and more responsible in many aspects of family living. As pupils achieve somewhat greater maturity, they are more ready to look ahead realistically to the kinds of homes they will establish later and to the local, state, and national situations affecting families.

Because the family is such a crucial element in the development of individuals, insights and abilities which can be developed to assist students in participating in, and later in establishing and maintaining, the kinds of families that help to create quality in our society are of great importance to the nation. Since most youth are members of family groups and will establish homes, the differing needs of individuals should be considered in planning and carrying out the program—those of the gifted student, the slow learner, the college-bound student, the potential dropout, and the student preparing for the more immediate vocation of homemaking.

CHAPTER IV

Content of the Curriculum

Awareness of the stage of development of individual pupils, their concerns, their backgrounds, and the impact of the environment on them is only part of the base a home economics teacher uses in guiding pupils at junior and senior high school levels. She also needs to be fully aware of the possibilities within each aspect of home economics for helping pupils to become more thoughtful, more capable, and more socially sensitive members of families and, thus, of the community.

Some aspects of home economics may appear in a program as a separate unit or course; some may be so interwoven with others that their individual contribution may not be apparent to the casual observer. Many times consumer education, management, home art, and family and social relationships are taught as integral parts of other units or courses. Each of these, for example, may be important considerations in a course which deals with the house and its furnishings and equipment. Or, in other circumstances, these may receive little or no attention. Even when these problems are considered as part of other courses, it may be important to bring the parts together and supplement them by focusing attention on such matters as family and social relations, management, consumer education, and so on. The importance of relationships, management, and consumer competence in modern family living is causing some teachers to focus attention on these problems, bringing in child development with family and social relations and considering food, clothing, shelter, and family health as part of management and consumer education. Since this chapter is concerned, not with how home economics is organized and taught, but rather with the scope the teacher uses as a base from which to choose, each aspect will be considered separately.

State Curricula Developed
by Secondary School Teachers

For many years state supervisors of home economics have used curriculum study as one basis for guiding the professional growth of teachers. Usually secondary school teachers have been assisted by representatives of the higher institutions in the state. Teacher educators have sometimes been consultants for curriculum committees and sometimes chairmen of statewide studies. College home economics teachers have served as consultants to secondary school teachers to make sure the subject matter has taken cognizance of the latest findings of research. As basic considerations, teachers have frequently studied the developmental tasks of youth and changes in society in general (and in the state in particular) which affect homes, pupil concerns, and home responsibilities. They have then developed resource materials for teacher use which the state departments of education have published and distributed. These guides have included sections on such items as over-all goals for home economics; objectives for different areas and school levels; suggested kinds of pupil experiences to attain these objectives; generalizations, principles, or basic learnings [1] likely to emerge; possible ways to evaluate pupil growth; and lists of source materials for teacher and pupil use.

The resource materials are expected to be used by teachers with discrimination in helping pupils of differing abilities, backgrounds, and interests and at various secondary school levels. Seldom would all that is included on a given phase of home economics be taught as organized in the guide in any one school. However, exceptional pupils with strong interests in certain phases might go beyond what is included in these guides.

Since these state resource materials have been developed by secondary school teachers after experience and careful study, they are used in this chapter to indicate scope of content.[2] There are a number of ways in which content is indicated: as a statement of objec-

---

[1] The term *learnings* or *basic learnings* is used in several guides and usually includes concepts, generalizations, principles, important facts, and key ideas.

[2] The illustrations included in this chapter have been selected from curriculum guides and other resource materials published and distributed by the Colorado, Indiana, Iowa, Louisiana, Oklahoma, Pennsylvania, West Virginia, and Wyoming State Departments of Education.

tives or outcomes for a given aspect; as an outline of subject matter; or as a statement of basic learnings or generalizations which pupils would be likely to glean from their experiences with the subject matter. Because of the frequency with which the terms *learnings* and *generalizations* are used, a word of caution is necessary in looking at the illustrations which follow. Sometimes these terms are used as a rule, a definition, or a list of factors; these are more likely to be used with beginning secondary school pupils. At other times, more fundamental relationships or generalizations are stated as learnings (see pp. 63–64). The more fundamental relationships are the ones the teacher seeks to help pupils find.

Because these guides are resource materials, it has been necessary, in order not to make this section too comprehensive, to select only a small portion of the material included for each aspect so as to give a general idea of the over-all scope. Details of subject matter and related concepts and generalizations have necessarily been omitted.

Content in Aspects of Home Economics

Art in the home and environment.   This is one aspect of home economics which is now seldom distinguished from others. The reasons lie in the changing school situation. In the early years of vocational education many schools had no art courses or, if they did, drawing, design, and composition were taught in such a way that pupils were unable to use them in achieving beauty in clothing or in the immediate environment. Since 1935, the schools have realized more clearly the important place of art in their programs. It is now more likely that home economics pupils will have gained some understanding of art principles. Home economics teachers, therefore, can give their attention to helping pupils apply these principles in the house and its furnishings, in clothing, and in other aspects of home living.

Child development.   The reasons given in one of the state bulletins for including child development in the homemaking program are:

> We believe that understanding children helps an individual
>   understand himself and others and thus makes possible self-
>   direction and self-discipline

understand and appreciate others
become a happier, more useful citizen in a democratic society
develop mutually satisfying relations with children

The bulletin lists some of the basic learnings which might result from the teaching of child development to pupils in early adolescence, with a focus on getting acquainted with and enjoying children; in middle adolescence, with a focus on understanding and guiding the growing child; and in later adolescence, with a focus on the baby and the family. A few of the anticipated learnings at these three stages suggest the content to be taught.

In early adolescence

Play is one means by which the child learns
Children are individuals; no two are alike in the way they develop or in the way they behave
Play materials contribute to the physical, mental, and social development of children
A child learns most effectively when he is free to make his own discoveries, mistakes, and decisions consistent with his level of development
Small children are curious. Their curiosity has to be channeled so that they do not hurt themselves nor are unduly destructive
Children are not born "good or bad"; they learn behavior.

Middle adolescence

Each child has his own rate, pattern, and ultimate level of development
Behavior is an indicator of a child's emotional development
There is always a reason why a child acts as he does
Desirable habits are developed when a child is mature enough, is interested, is successful, and accepts the learning
The development of a child is influenced by the physical and emotional care provided by his environment
The community has a responsibility toward children.

Later adolescence

The values of family life often change when children come into the family
The prenatal growth and the birth of a baby follow a pattern
Adequate prenatal care assures health during pregnancy and childbirth
The care the baby gets during his first year largely determines his future development
The family is an important social group in formulating the attitudes of the individual, in meeting his basic needs, and in forming his personality patterns.

Satisfactory relationships with children are dependent on mutual affection, enjoyment, and respect of the adult and child

There are many agencies interested in the problems of children and willing to supply information about their care.

One notes that the learnings tend to involve somewhat deeper understanding in the more advanced stages of development. In middle adolescent development, for example, the pupils merely recognize that the community has responsibility toward children. In later adolescence, the pupils would have had a number of pertinent experiences before coming to the conclusion regarding agencies interested in children; they may have read pamphlets about the work of different community agencies, or heard welfare workers describe the purposes and activities of their agencies, or visited some of the agencies in the community concerned with children.

Clothing and textiles. In early adolescence the emphasis suggested in some of the state curriculum guides includes such topics as:

Grooming of the adolescent—health habits, care of the complexion, hair, and body

Selection of such clothing as shoes, dresses, undergarments for school

Daily and weekly care of clothing, including removal of spots and stains, simple repairs, and laundering such articles as sweaters

Choosing cotton fabrics, considering color, design, wearability, care required

Choosing a pattern for a garment suited to the individual and her skills

Choosing tools and equipment, using them effectively, and caring for them

Establishing efficient work habits

Making a simple garment including learning to adjust a pattern, preparing a fabric for cutting, interpreting pattern instruction sheet and symbols, pinning and cutting, marking construction details, assembling garment.

In adolescence, some of the emphasis is on these topics:

Planning a wardrobe for a season, considering family funds for clothing

Selection of colors and designs suited to the individual

Purchase of such garments as coat, sweater, skirt

Major characteristics of fibers, weaves, and finishes of fabrics

Shopping practices, use of labels, the Labelling Act, kinds of stores

Scientific advances in clothing care—soaps and detergents, effects of heat, moisture, pressure on different fabrics

Simple alteration and repair of ready-to-wear garments

Making a garment of more difficult material and/or design—selection of pattern, fabric, altering pattern, fitting and assembling garment (set-in sleeves, collars and cuffs, accessories, linings), organizing equipment and tools for efficient work.

This kind of emphasis in the selecting and making of clothing provides opportunity to give pupils help with some of their planning and purchasing problems, assumes they have developed an understanding of some of the art principles and builds on these, and provides some understanding of clothing care and construction. There is limited emphasis on family clothing problems. If more time were devoted to clothing, these—along with the social, economic, psychological, and creative aspects of clothing—would have more attention.

Consumer education. Helping pupils with consumer buying problems is a normal part of work in foods, clothing, health, housing, but many schools find it important to give additional attention to other over-all consumer considerations of importance to families. The ability to buy wisely is as important an economic contribution to a family as the ability to earn. The amount of advertising directed to the teen-age consumer and the amount of money many teen-agers have to spend make it doubly important that young people acquire as good a basis as possible for making their purchasing decisions. It has been estimated that, through earnings, allowances, gifts, and other sources of funds, adolescents in the United States spend a total of nine or ten billion dollars annually. Much of this money is spent on impulse or irresponsible buying.

State home economics curriculum guides tend to emphasize, for the young adolescent, the management of pocket money and the buying of specific types of products; for the middle adolescent, the problems of managing family income and an evaluation of sources of information as guides for buying; for the later adolescent, an analysis of the relationships between the consumer, the market, and those agencies concerned with consumer protection. Some of the learnings or generalizations selected from curriculum guides indicate content:

A person's true values are usually reflected in the way he spends his money

A record of expenditures provides a basis for analysis and planning what one desires for money spent

Choices made every day determine the kind of life one builds for himself

A systematic plan for saving and spending assures a more balanced distribution of one's money among needs and wants

Purchases made by individuals help to determine the quality and kind of products and services available

Distributing the family income among necessities such as food, clothing, shelter, medical care, insurance, and individual needs and wants involves careful planning

Advertising which is informative and truthful helps the buyer, while half-truths and emotional appeals may mislead him

Factual information on labels helps the buyer and will be improved if the consumer demands it

Knowing specific standards and items covered in guarantees, warranties, seals of approval, and trademarks determines the amount of dependence to be placed on them when buying

Agencies' research reports on commodities can be helpful to the consumer

An analysis of total costs of credit, installment buying, or loans balanced against needs and income helps in determining whether any of these should be used

Selecting places to buy involves determining kinds and amounts of services as well as goods one wishes to pay for

Savings and insurance can be a means of achieving long-time goals and a cushion against the unexpected and emergencies

Income, standard of living, willingness to take risks, and age influence the amount and kind of insurance to purchase

Knowing advantages and disadvantages of bank services, government bonds, postal savings, savings and loan associations, stocks and bonds, real estate helps a family evaluate which are adapted to their needs

Decisions made about the use of resources when the United States was isolated differ from those called for in "One World"

The concern of the individual for incomes and living conditions in other countries as well as his own helps to determine kinds of purchases to make and uses to which taxes are allocated

Local, state, and federal taxes make possible the purchase of services, protection, education, recreation, research, regulations, inspection, which would be difficult or more expensive for the individual family to provide.

Helping pupils to acquire these and related understandings and to act on them is facilitated when other units in the home economics program have given attention to buying and to other economic considerations and when cooperative planning for these learnings is possible between home economics teachers and other teachers in a given school (see pp. 79–80).

Family and social relationships.   The results of committee work by home economics teachers with assistance in a workshop, as published in one state, include "some possible learnings" in personal and family relationships. The content suggested for the eighth grade deals with "understanding and accepting body changes and how these affect one's feelings" and "living with family and friends." For the ninth grade, the focus is on "understanding ourselves and others." For the tenth grade, the emphasis is on "growing toward maturity." For the eleventh and twelfth grades, the focus is on "looking toward the future." Selections from the possible learnings indicate the emphases in different grades:

Eighth grade

The kind of individual one becomes depends upon his heredity, his environment and upon his determination to become his best self

The body changes during adolescence are a part of growing up; every adolescent has to accept and make adjustments to these changes

As one grows up mentally, emotionally, and socially, he learns to take more responsibility, set standards for his own conduct, and solve his problems

Families can provide, in addition to physical needs, love, security, and a sense of belonging

Each member of the family has some responsibilities as well as some privileges

Observing family customs and traditions is one way to help strengthen family unity

Some conflict is normal in any family

Good manners are based upon kindness, consideration, and respect

Showing an interest in people of all ages enriches one's life

The more varied one's interests, the more likely that one's circle of friends will increase

Parents are naturally concerned about their sons' and daughters' friends because friends have great influence over one's thinking and behavior.

Ninth grade

Understanding reasons for feelings and actions helps one understand and get along with others

Growth and development go on as long as an individual strives to improve and becomes increasingly mature in the way he faces and reacts to life

The mature person keeps within bounds of behavior approved by society

Differences are more easily resolved when all concerned can talk freely about the issues involved

In the democratic family there is mutual acceptance and support; each member has a right to be heard, to have his values respected and his feelings accepted

Family loyalties are built through mutual thoughtfulness and a growing unity.

Tenth grade

Understanding what is important in life and planning a course of action based on such values contributes to a satisfying and worthwhile life

Personal actions reflect upon the family

Assuming increasing responsibility for one's behavior and accepting the consequences shows growth toward maturity

The mature person thinks in terms of long-time as well as immediate goals.

Eleventh and twelfth grades

Homemaking is a career that is stimulating and rewarding to the extent that it involves creativity and satisfying results

A young person needs to be concerned not only with making a good choice but also with being the kind of person who will be a good marriage partner

Marriage is successful to the extent that each works to make it so

Marriage is a partnership which may be strengthened as conflicts in interests, loyalties, and values are resolved together

Successful family living, like any other kind of continuing happiness, is never achieved with finality but is always a matter of day-to-day and year-to-year achievement

Families make up the community and have responsibilities for making it a desirable place to live.

This last learning suggests a part of family and social relationships too often neglected. Some of the state curriculum guides give a desirable emphasis to the contributions made by different agencies and organizations in the community, to an analysis of their policies and costs, and to gaps in services families need.

Food and nutrition.   To indicate the scope of food and nutrition, objectives have been selected from resource materials developed by teachers in one state under nutrition, meal planning, selection and buying of food, storage, preparation, meal service, manners and entertaining, preservation and conservation of food, sanitation, safety and management. Some of the topics and objectives have been combined in this selection:

Nutrition

Acceptance of high nutrition standards to serve as a guide in selection of foods

Understanding that an adequate diet includes the essential nutrients for maximum development and maintenance of the body

Some knowledge of the effects of food handling, manufacturing, processing, and methods of production on nutritive content of foods

Understanding and willingness to practice food habits that are conducive to optimum health

Understanding that solving nutrition problems may assist in bringing world peace

A continuing interest in recent research findings and scientific developments relating to nutrition

Ability to plan simple meals using accepted principles of meal planning.

Selection, buying, and storage

Ability to buy nutritionally adequate food within the family's food budget

Knowledge of the marketing facilities in a local community

Ability to use labels, brands, grades, and prices as guides in buying

Understanding of the food laws and regulations—local, state, and federal—which protect the consumer

Understanding the relationship between health and proper sanitation in food handling

Knowledge of the care and storage needed to retain food nutrients.

Preparation and management

Interest in preparing foods

Ability to identify, use, and care for food preparation equipment

Interest in establishing good working relations with others

Ability to adjust and follow a recipe satisfactorily

Ability to prepare palatable, nutritious meals

Development of good work habits

An understanding of good safety practices in the preparation of foods

Ability to use efficient management practices in planning, preparing, and serving meals.

Preservation and conservation

Some understanding of the world's food problems and the relationship of food to national security

Desire to prevent food waste

Ability to select foods for preservation and to preserve them in different ways.

An analysis of these objectives convinces one that some are adapted to more advanced pupils and some are useful with junior high school pupils. This publication suggests that, for early adolescence the emphasis be on helping with family meals, sanitation, work habits, individual and group work, use of recipes and equipment, use of time, and the contribution of foods to personal appearance and health. For middle adolescence, the emphasis proposed is on planning, preparing, and serving meals, meeting food needs of the family, selecting food, planning menus, buying foods, and preserving and conserving food. In later adolescence, emphasis would be given to other nutrition problems, to the dangers involved in food fads and fallacies; to factors involved in the production and marketing of food which affect costs and qualities; to protection through laws, regulation, and inspection; and to food problems of other countries and the relation of these to world peace.

Health, home nursing, and safety. The mimeographed bulletin used for this aspect of home economics includes material on safety precautions at home, personal and family health, first aid, community health and safety, civil defense, home nursing, mental attitudes and happiness, and family health economics. Selections from "understandings, principles, generalizations" are given in the sequence in which they might be taught; starting with early adolescence.

An understanding of some of the signs of illness may prevent development of a more complicated type of illness

Checking homes for possible accident hazards may prevent serious accidents

Correct use of equipment will prevent minor or more serious accidents

An understanding and use of the available health agencies will help in improving the health of a community

Communicable diseases spread rapidly if allowed to go unchecked

Proper immunization will prevent some diseases as smallpox, diphtheria and poliomyelitis

Improvised equipment can add to the comfort of the patient

A patient who is provided a means of self-entertainment will usually be more contented

When a person buys a health insurance policy, he should "shop" for the one which will really be most beneficial to him

Public health is a community effort to prevent disease, to prolong life, and to promote mental and physical efficiency

Voluntary health agencies are largely dependent on volunteer help and are supported by contributions.

These understandings start with some of the ideas young people can put into operation and move on to some which more directly involve the family and, later, those concerned with the community. In some situations, the national and international aspects of health may well be emphasized.

Housing of the family. A state curriculum committee made up of teachers, teacher educators, and supervisors of home economics suggests that the emphasis for early adolescence be on planning a comfortable, convenient, attractive room for oneself; for middle adolescence, on improving living areas; for late adolescence, on housing problems of young people:

For early adolescence

Privacy is important to each individual and should be provided for even in shared bedrooms

Planning together for the use and care of a shared room helps to prevent conflict between family members

Large pieces of furniture should be parallel with the wall

Free circulation of air and heat should be considered in furniture arrangement

A specific place to store all items helps to maintain order

A pleasing color scheme adds much to the attractiveness of a bedroom.

For middle adolescence

The attractiveness of any area depends on the shape and placement of objects, colors, designs, and textures

Objects in a room need to be related in form and shape to create a feeling of unity and harmony

Two or more colors appear more attractive when used in different shades and in different degrees of brightness or dullness

Floor coverings are important in correlating home furnishings

A variety of textures helps to make a room attractive, when they are harmonious with each other and with the colors, materials, shapes, lines, and patterns in the area

In selecting cleaning equipment that will be useful for more than one task, consideration of its efficiency, ease of operation, care required, and cost will result in a more satisfactory choice

A home can be attractively furnished at minimum cost with a plan for additions and improvements

The largest part of the furnishing budget should be spent on articles that receive constant wear, provide physical comfort, and are likely to be suitable if moved to a new setting.

For later adolescence

Important factors to consider in selecting a place to live are: present family income, permanency of location, permanency of income, furniture and housekeeping needs, security for other financial needs

A family that rents has somewhat greater freedom to move and possible greater economy in day-to-day living, but also possible insecurity, impersonality of surroundings, and unsatisfactory terms of lease

Advantages of owning a home are security, family solidarity, respect for and understanding of the value of property, and owning an investment. The disadvantages are having a large share of family income in shelter, unpredictable expenses, increased responsibility, and possibility of loss

Costs of financing a home vary with the source from which money is borrowed as well as the home chosen

Kitchens are more convenient when equipment is grouped according to centers of use. These can be roughly divided into several categories: planning, preparation, serving, dining, cleaning, storage

With thought and effort the family can modify even the most inconveniently planned areas to serve its present needs

Landscape design is a matter of strengthening the relationship between the family and the land. Planning before planting may help avoid costly mistakes.

These aspects of housing do not include any consideration of community housing problems, such as the relation of the individual house to the neighborhood, zoning laws and their purpose in a locality, or the extent to which families in the community have adequate or inadequate housing. Eliminated also are means of meeting the housing needs of low-income families, contrasts in housing problems in different climates, and differences between developing countries and already developed ones. These too are issues to which young people should give some thought in home economics or other courses.

Management. It is not likely that other phases of home economics will be taught without some consideration of the management problems involved. It is, however, questionable whether the amount of management which is important in modern living is usually included. The term *management* is used here to indicate the means by which individuals and families use their resources (material goods, money, credit, time, special abilities and skills, knowledge, mental and physical energy, interests and attitudes, community facilities) to attain their goals and values; that is, how they work to achieve the kind of life they want most. Management involves planning, making decisions, and organizing and coordinating efforts in carrying out decisions. Unfortunately the term *home management* has often been misused as a title for a course which is not concerned with management but, rather, with a consideration of other aspects such as the house, its furnishing and equipment, family health, laundering, and cleaning.

Although the early adolescent may need help with decisions regarding the use of one resource such as time or money, it is important that pupils come to recognize the interrelation among resources and grow in ability to direct their choices by clearly defined goals and values. Pupils at the early adolescent age may try out two or three ways to save time and energy on a specific job, such as making a bed or organizing a drawer or storage cabinet. They may learn to keep records of money spent, to analyze whether they are getting most satisfaction from expenditures, to plan and carry out a revised plan. But the management job is more complex and they need to develop an ability to recognize the various alternative resources, to be aware of the values determining their choices, and to take account of the effects of their decisions on others as well as themselves.

Some of the learnings in several of the curriculum guides have been selected to illustrate those developed with early and middle adolescents:

A plan for spending makes it possible to get more satisfaction for one's money

Each individual has his own goals to serve as a guide for the use of money

A work schedule adapted to the individual can help save time and energy

Storing articles used together in the place of first and most frequent use can save time

Standards vary from one home to another depending on which values are important to the families involved

When all members help in keeping the standards set by the family, no one is likely to have too heavy a load

A well-managed home contributes to the optimum development of its members

Recognition of the needs of each family member is basic in the sharing of resources.

Laura Kivlin distributed to home economics teachers in the secondary schools in one state a list of learnings in home management and asked them to check off those which they were teaching. Some of the important learnings in management teaching were:

Values are components of life which an individual considers basically worthwhile. For example, good health, family well-being, education, and development of all family members; security; beauty; participation in church and community activities; and a comfortable home

There is no right way in which any resource should be used. An individual's or family's use of resources depends on values, goals, standards, and specific circumstances in which the individual or family lives

The diversity of cultural backgrounds in the United States—as represented by traditional holidays, foods, clothing, and artifacts—provides opportunity for enrichment of life

Community resources such as streets, police and fire protection, schools, churches, libraries, stores, parks, and hospitals are definite resources for families who otherwise would have to provide them for themselves at greater cost . . .

In choosing equipment, a person should consider not only the initial cost but also the alternative of hiring the job done, the time and energy it will save, the frequency of use and the amount of care, maintenance, and storage space required

It is imperative to count the opportunity cost in determining the total cost of home-produced items—that is, what other use would be made of the time, energy, equipment, skills, and knowledge if they were not used in making things

The reasons for trying to simplify work (being more effective or efficient) are: to be able to accomplish the necessary tasks without fatigue; to have time and energy for other activities with the family, for the community, or for one's pleasure and development

Correct working heights reduce the amount of energy necessary to do a task

Frequent short rest periods help one to recover from fatigue more rapidly than infrequent longer ones

Goals need to be realistic and should be selected with regard to the family's values, the availability of resources and all demands on these resources . . .

Flexible standards, to fit changing situations, almost always result in more happiness and satisfaction for the family than too high or too rigid ones . . .

Good family and personal relationships are often the solution to many of the most difficult home management problems. Likewise, good home management for better relationships.[3]

---

[3] Laura Douglas Kivlin, "The Beliefs and Reported Practices of Two Groups of Pennsylvania Homemaking Teachers in the Area of Home Management" (University Park, Pa.: Ed.D. dissertation presented at Pennsylvania State University, 1962).

In the state Kivlin studied, reports indicated that a significant proportion of home economics teachers did not include alternative use of resources, possibilities of increasing resources, and individual responsibility for contributions to community resources. She found, also, that use of credit, insurance, social security, and income taxes, although pertinent considerations, were frequently neglected in dealing with family financial planning. There is no reason to believe that these findings would be very different in other states. Home economics teachers may well give more emphasis to the kind of management these learnings of Kivlin's suggest.

Use of State Resource Materials in Local Schools

Such resource materials, a small part of which have been illustrated, must be thoughtfully used if they are to serve the purpose they are intended to serve. They are of value in helping to call to mind the elements of different aspects of home economics which might be taught. Helping to develop such resource materials can also be one of the effective forms of in-service education and encourages the critical use of such materials later.

In studying the basis for the sequence of learning proposed in these state guides, one notes a tendency to focus work for early adolescents on understanding oneself and becoming a helpful member of the family. For middle adolescents, the emphasis is generally on developing some independence from the family and assuming responsibilities in the family and social group. For later adolescents, emphasis tends to be on growing into maturity, looking toward the future, and carrying responsibility in the community. These, however, are very general emphases; the understanding, attitudes, and abilities of individual members will help to determine the sequence chosen.

In setting up priorities with pupils in their classes, teachers will be evaluating (a) the types of pupils, their backgrounds, their stages of development, their purposes (both immediate and long-range), (b) the home economics courses they have already taken and those they are likely to take, (c) the time limitations of each course, (d) the content in such courses as science, social science, and art which can supplement and strengthen pupils' learning in home economics. A balancing of all these factors should result in an emphasis that will be a challenge to the abilities of students.

Concepts and Generalizations

Because the teacher knows that more permanent and useful learning results when pupils have gone beyond acquiring many detailed facts and have been brought to the stage of synthesizing these into concepts or generalizations,[4] she will ask herself which of these concepts or generalizations are important for specific groups of pupils. Concepts, as names or phrases which help to organize ideas, events, or objects, are useful in providing some kind of framework or structure into which details can be fitted. Some of the concepts which pupils would probably derive during their study of home economics would be concerned with the place of the family in our society, similarities and differences in values and goals of different families, the family life cycle, basic needs of infants and small children, roles of individuals in families, consumer competence, and resources available to families.

Generalizations and conclusions drawn from many detailed facts express an underlying truth and usually state or imply relationships among these facts. Because these relationships, too, are general, they help to supply a framework and can be useful in new situations. As one looks over the learnings listed in this chapter, it is apparent that these differ appreciably among themselves in the extent of generalization.

Three general kinds of learnings can be distinguished. The first involves those learnings which are primarily directions to be followed; for example: "Large pieces of furniture should be parallel with the wall," or "Free circulation of air and heat should be considered in furniture arrangement." It may be helpful at times to have rules to follow, but if the reasons for the procedure were made clear, the pupil would be able to be more independent in deciding what to do in a new situation. Other statements do indicate relationships: "A specific place to store all items helps to maintain order," or "Objects in a room need to be related in form and shape to create a feeling of harmony."

---

[4] Ralph Garry, *The Psychology of Learning* (Washington, D.C.: The Center for Applied Research in Education, Inc., 1963), p. 49.

Another type of learning is a definition, description, or a list of factors to consider. Such a learning may or may not indicate relationships; for example: "Public health is a community effort to prevent disease, to prolong life, and to promote mental and physical efficiency." Such a definition may be very important for pupils considering individual and group responsibility for health; it might be called a concept. Another example: "In the democratic family there is mutual acceptance and support; each member has a right to be heard, to have his values respected, and to have his feelings accepted." This description of a democratic family could be a conclusion from many experiences. It implies a relationship between democracy and these factors.

A third type of learning either states a relationship or implies it. It expresses an underlying truth as, for example: "Play is one means by which a child learns." This relation between learning and play could be very meaningful to a junior high school pupil when observing a child or selecting a toy for one. "Price is not necessarily an indication of quality" can serve as a guide whenever one shops and could have been a conclusion from a series of experiences with many types of goods.

To help pupils understand concepts and generalizations likely to be useful in home living, the teacher provides opportunities for experiences involving the same general idea so that relationships become apparent and conclusions can be drawn. The level at which an individual pupil can arrive at these concepts and generalizations depends on the number of facts at his disposal, his past and present experiences, his maturity, and his ability to do reflective and somewhat more abstract thinking. The younger pupils may state the general idea quite simply; then, as they gain further experience and see other applications, they may be more precise in the conclusions they draw. Even though a generalization is stated in the same manner by a younger student and by a more experienced pupil, the wider experience of the latter should have brought out a greater realization of the implications of the statement and of its complexity.

This chapter is not intended to indicate what schools teach or should teach in a specific situation. It does suggest, however, the scope which would be considered by teachers as they work with secondary school pupils. It also suggests that the more successful teachers are those who decide to concentrate on developing with pupils the most important concepts and generalizations in modern home living, rather than those who try to include all the facts or skills that might conceivably be useful to pupils. Whatever the aspect of home economics on which pupils are concentrating, the success of the teacher is to a large extent dependent on her grasp of general principles of learning.

CHAPTER V

Applying Principles of Learning in Home Economics Instruction

The manner in which a teacher works with pupils in the classroom is as important, if not more important, than the subject content of the program. Neither can be considered lightly. In fact, Symonds' review of research in *What Education Has to Learn from Psychology* led him to say:

> The evidence is conclusive and the conclusion is inescapable that one does not achieve mental power by means of a particular subject of study. Mental power—intelligence—if it can be achieved through study must come not by virtue of the *subject matter* but through the *methods* employed and hence learned. Mental growth depends primarily on how a subject is taught and on the emphasis in its teaching.[1]

This means that in viewing such aspects of home economics as are considered in the preceding chapter, the home economics teacher must ask not only *what* is most important for the pupils in a particular class, but also *how* she can work with them in such a way as to develop their mental powers? What methods are adapted to members of this group? How can she teach so that, as they meet new situations in their home living, they will proceed intelligently, using the background of knowledge, skills, and methods of thinking to which they have become accustomed in their home economics classes?

Kinds of Experiences in Home Economics

Before considering how home economics is and may be taught, two types of experiences which are used by home economics teachers in addition to those in the classroom need to be mentioned.

---

[1] Percival M. Symonds, *What Education Has to Learn from Psychology* (New York: Teachers College, Bureau of Publications, Columbia University, 1959), p. 81.

In home and community. For many years teachers have encouraged home economics pupils to repeat at home processes learned at school so that they might develop some skill in the real situation at home. With the beginning of the vocational program in home economics, emphasis was placed on a more comprehensive kind of experience in the home in which the pupil undertakes a project with specific goals in mind for further learning, using information and abilities acquired at school and extending these as needed.[2] For example, the pupil interested in rearranging or redecorating her room learns at school about possible arrangements and color schemes for different settings and clarifies some generalizations to guide her solution of particular problems. Her experience at home will be likely to include considering with family members what might be done, discussing the amount of money and time which could be allocated to the project, perhaps inviting the teacher and other members of the class to visit and offer suggestions, and deciding upon a plan which is feasible. Carrying out the plan helps her to apply school learnings to a specific situation, calls for cooperation with family members in considering their values and goals, and often raises new problems which demand further study at school. Since many activities which were formerly confined to the home are now commercial, group, or community endeavors, community projects sometimes carried through as club projects are, like home and classroom projects, a part of the pupils' learning experiences.

Through club projects. For some time home economics clubs were a local school development; then, in several states, a statewide program was developed. Later, clubs were organized on a national basis as The Future Homemakers of America (FHA). As an integral part of the school program in home economics, chapters of the FHA offer opportunities for the further development of pupil initiative in carrying out activities related to homemaking. They stress the importance of the homemaker's contribution to the home and the community. Stimulation for assuming these responsibilities comes from the program of work which is developed by the members.

---

[2] Druzilla Kent, *et al., Home, School, and Community Experiences in the Homemaking Program,* U.S. Department of Health, Education and Welfare, Vocational Division Bulletin No. 252 (Washington, D.C.: USGPO, 1957).

The over-all goal—"to help individuals improve personal, family, and community living"—serves as a guide to the program of work developed every three years by the national organization for use by state and local chapters. Four objectives are included in the 1962– 65 program, each with one or two projects and suggested chapter and individual experiences. The objectives and projects were:

Objectives	*Projects*
Discovering myself and my worth to others	You and Your Values
Contributing to the joys and satisfactions of family living	Focus on Family Friendship Marriage Calls for Preparation
Strengthening my education for future roles	Stay in School
Launching good citizenship through homemaking	Action for Citizenship [3]

Principles as Criteria

To evaluate the ways in which home economics is taught in the classroom, and through home, community, and club projects, some criteria are needed. One basis for such criteria may well be statements of principles of learning which have appeared in books and magazines during the 1950's and 1960's. The review of research by Symonds, already referred to, contains many useful statements. *The Psychology of Learning,* by Garry,[4] not only includes statements of principles but also discusses their application to the learner, the learning task, and teaching procedures. Fifty statements by Watson of "what we really know today about children and learning," with which the author believes "few knowledgeable psychologists of any 'school' would disagree"[5] is another source. A few of these statements, together with samples of home economics teaching, are discussed in this chapter and indicate the usefulness of such principles as criteria.

Participation in planning. Watson says: *"Children are more*

---

[3] Future Homemakers cf America, *National Program of Work, 1962–1965* (Washington 25, D.C.: Office of Education, Department of Health, Education and Welfare, n.d.).

[4] Ralph Garry, *The Psychology of Learning* (Washington, D.C.: The Center for Applied Research in Education, Inc., 1963).

[5] Goodwin Watson, *What Psychology Can We Trust?* (New York: Teachers College, Bureau of Publications, Columbia University, 1961).

apt to throw themselves wholeheartedly into any project if they themselves have participated in the selection and planning of the enterprise. Genuine participation (not pretended sharing) has been found to increase motivation, adaptability, and speed of learning." [6] As for the opposite kind of teacher activity: *"Reaction to excessive direction by the teacher is likely to be (a) apathetic conformity, (b) defiance, (c) scapegoating, or (d) escape from the whole affair."*

The curriculum guides consulted in securing illustrations for the preceding chapter quite generally suggested that time be taken during the early part of the year or semester to plan with the pupils, to help them set goals and decide upon some of the types of experiences they need to attain the goals. Teacher educators usually try to provide such experiences in planning with pupils as a part of student teaching.

Because home economics deals with personal and home responsibilities undertaken frequently, it is easy to plan with pupils what is to be done. To illustrate, one teacher of an eighth-grade class heard her pupils discussing their babysitting experiences. Entering the conversation, she learned that 80 per cent of them were taking care of children two to eight years old and that they were having some problems they didn't know how to meet. Inquiry revealed that they would like help with these problems. The teacher's suggestions of some books and magazine articles to read and a visit to a kindergarten to see how a teacher dealt with some of the problems presented by this age group were readily accepted. Their further study helped them to make out an observation sheet to use during the visit to the kindergarten. They planned with the teacher for their part as visitors. An analysis of the observation sheets after the visit helped pupils to draw a few conclusions about the interests of children and the kinds of relationships that might be established with them. This led to a further study of stories, toys, and games suitable for children of different ages. With the help of some parents, they developed an instruction sheet with information needed for babysitting and suggestions of things to do if an emergency arose. Later a children's party at school was planned and carried

---

[6] *Ibid.,* p. 5.
[7] *Ibid.,* p. 5.

out and this helped in a further analysis of children's interests, re-actions, and abilities, and in their own relations to children.

It is important to emphasize that planning with pupils does not mean that the teacher should do no preliminary planning. An acquaintance with individual pupils and a knowledge of their personal and home situations provides a basis for thinking through what their purposes might well be and what kinds of experiences might be helpful in attaining those purposes. It also helps the teacher get together materials for pupil use. One teacher reported:

> Being new to the community this year, determining the needs of my students and their families was my first problem. Autobiographies, checklists, informal discussions, and reaction sheets were used to gather information from my students. Permanent school records, test scores, and the guidance department were helpful. The results of the survey done in the schools was an excellent source of information. Valuable also was the information and attitudes revealed through discussions with other teachers, parents, and friends of students.

With such preparation the teacher is able to supplement the goals and suggested experiences stated by pupils and help them evaluate many possibilities before deciding what is needed.

Planning with pupils does not mean persuading them to adopt purposes the teacher has thought through. It may involve teaching pupils how to plan, how to clarify goals, how to evaluate possible ways of working, and how to decide what may be done by the whole group and what may be done by small groups or by individuals. The report of an Oregon teacher of her work with forty-four juniors and seniors in one high school indicates that the class started out by listing problems of family members and then organized these and decided which they had a basis for solving and which they needed to study further. This enabled them to set their goals for the year. They then decided upon classroom standards and operating procedures which became guideposts to learning. Because individuals had somewhat different needs, the students divided themselves into groups with similar or related goals. Time was taken for the groups to consider together what makes for good group relations, effective committee work, and a good learning experience. The groups as a whole had an experience in the process of problem-solving. Each group then clarified its goals, set up a plan of work for the year, and proceeded to work (individually and in committees) with a good deal of independence (see also p. 81).[8]

This Oregon teacher provided a base for effective independent work, after the project was selected and planned, by taking time to develop the understandings and skills needed. Some of the skills which may be important include the ability to find pertinent and authoritative source materials, the ability to prepare for field trips or interviews and evaluate them afterwards, the ability to use a film or filmstrip critically, the ability to interpret or make tables or charts, the ability to lead a group, and the ability to be an effective member of a committee. Taking time to develop these skills is an important part of the *methods* which Symonds points out are so vital to mental growth.

Cooperation for a common goal. The title of the Oregon teacher's report, and her own analysis of what she did, include the words *cooperative planning.* How important is cooperative planning? Watson says:

> *When groups act for a common goal there is better cooperation and more friendliness than when individuals in the group are engaged in competitive rivalry with one another.* Some studies indicate that the more cooperative groups also produce results of better quality. The competitive emphasis directs attention toward winning rather than toward excellence of performance.[9]

Throughout the Oregon teacher's report, the cooperative elements are indicated: the whole class assisted in listing family problems; groups analyzed these to determine in what aspects of home economics they fell; groups planned what they should do to attain common goals; the whole class worked together to carry out certain projects; the group as a whole developed guideposts to learning; each member had an opportunity to serve as a member of a committee.

This principle of learning has been a part of good classroom work in home economics for some years. It has also been a guide in the activities of the FHA. Members and leaders of the organization, recognizing that homes flourish on cooperation rather than on

---

8 Mary Jane Grieve, *Cooperative Planning in an Advanced Homemaking Education Class* (Corvallis, Oregon: University Cooperative Association, P.O. Box 491, 1960), 26 pp.

9 Watson, *op. cit.,* p. 15. See also Garry, *op. cit.,* p. 74.

rivalry among members, decided that as future homemakers they needed to learn to cooperate with each other and with other groups. In 1960 they expressed their beliefs about this in a published bulletin entitled *Cooperative and Competitive Activities in Home Economics Education."* [10]

The home economics pupils in one Maryland school, some of whom were FHA members, became teen-age consumers by taking responsibility for buying small equipment and appliances for the kitchens in the new home economics department. A part of their FHA chapter report follows:

> The first step was to determine what was needed. We pored through catalogues, magazines and old inventories to compile our lists and set up criteria for selection. In our discussions, we learned that compromise is sometimes necessary, that the decision of the majority usually rules, and that advance planning is most helpful.
>
> When all groups were ready to shop, four local department stores and a china shop were chosen. Each store agreed to open a charge account for the Oxon Hill FHA chapter, for, although the County had set up the required appropriation, actual cash was not made available. In this way we learned procedures involved in buying on a charge account and the value of a good credit rating.
>
> All FHA members participated in the shopping trips. . . . Each FHA member had the responsibility of purchasing one or more items for the six kitchens.
>
> Through home economics magazines, we also became aware of the educational discounts offered to schools. So after comparison shopping in local stores, we ordered some of the electrical equipment and cooking utensils by mail at considerable savings. . . .
>
> During the second year of this project, another sum of $250.00 was made available to equip a home management unit. . . . The ease with which we could now go about making the necessary purchases showed we had made great progress toward learning "sense with dollars." [11]

In these situations, pupils were learning how to cooperate to achieve a common goal as they worked together to plan and carry out their class and chapter projects with the guidance of the home economics teacher and the club adviser (see also pp. 81 and 86).

Planning together for evaluation of results is another type of co-

---

[10] Future Homemakers of America, *Cooperative and Competitive Activities in Home Economics Education* (Washington, D.C.: Office of Education, Department of Health, Education and Welfare, n.d.).

[11] "Learning by Spending," *Teen Times,* Vol. 17, No. 2 (November, 1961), 14.

operative activity in which teacher, parents, and pupils engage. Clarifying goals and deciding on evidences to watch for in determining whether or not these goals are being attained are important parts of the educational experience. As pupils see results, they gain confidence in their ability and are encouraged to extend their efforts. Parents' comments are often helpful.

> Yesterday when we were looking for a skirt in the store, Alice examined each one carefully, noting workmanship, color in relation to other clothes she would wear with it, quality of material before deciding on a purchase.

A recent graduate said:

> I had planned to be married as soon as I finished school; but my senior home economics course opened up a whole new possibility to me and I am going on to college next year instead.

A teacher commented:

> To me, one of the most satisfying rewards of teaching home economics . . . has been my students going home and telling their mothers and neighbors what we did in class that day. Sometimes "my girls" will try to teach their mothers some of the various projects we are doing in class. Then when they go as far as they can, they bring the project to school for further help or the mother telephones about the next step.

These comments indicate characteristic attitudes and behavior of pupils. Other kinds of goals may be appraised in other ways; for example, knowledge and understanding of principles by objective type tests; skills, by performance tests; personal qualities, by other means.[12] The results found should be shared with pupils as soon as possible since "knowledge of results is as valuable as reward and goal-setting in its contribution to performance."[13]

Promoting thinking. Another principle of learning stated by Watson is illustrated by the way the pupils in the Maryland school proceeded:

---

[12] J. Stanley Ahmann, *Testing Student Achievements and Attitudes* (Washington, D.C.: The Center for Applied Research in Education, Inc., 1962); Henrietta Fleck *How to Evaluate Students* (Bloomington, Ill.: McKnight & McKnight Publishing Co., 1953); Merle E. Bonney and Richard S. Hampleman, *Personal-Social Evaluation Techniques* (Washington, D.C.: The Center for Applied Research in Education, 1962).

[13] Garry, *op. cit.*, p. 67.

Pupils think when they encounter an obstacle, difficulty, puzzle, or challenge in a course of action which interests them. The process of thinking involves designing and testing plausible solutions for the problem as understood by the thinker.[14]

The problem of the pupils in the Maryland school involved real difficulties and apparently served as a challenge to the members of this group. By the same token, the help given by the Oregon teacher on the process of problem-solving and the use of this process by individuals and groups furnished a basis for the development of the ability to think on the part of the members of that class. In all aspects of home economics there are problems in which most pupils are interested and in which they meet obstacles or difficulties which call for thinking. Many teachers begin a new semester or a new unit by having class members indicate difficulties they have or problems they recognize. The more important difficulties or problems are then used as a basis for the work.

One teacher, new to a Maine community, found that many of the mothers of her pupils were employed outside the home:

A large share of the homemaking responsibilities fall upon the teen-age student. Meal preparation, some shopping, and food selection seemed most often mentioned. The foods units in both classes were aimed at helping these girls make the best of what they had to work with and carry out responsibilities . . . for family meals considering costs, food budgeting, and ways to maintain nutritive values, learn short cuts, and manage time better.

Because mothers are working, care of the younger children may also fall to the teen-ager. The junior class child care units had a double purpose—to assist the girls with their problems in child care now and to prepare them for responsibilities as mothers of the future. (Many of these girls will be married before finishing school or soon thereafter.) Our classes were aimed at understanding the growth and development of children and fostering this through play, routine, and discipline. We climaxed this unit with a party for children aged two to five, borrowing and making play materials. . . . Each student made an observation on a selected child in his home and at the party and was responsible for some direct activity with a group of children. I feel the project was extremely valuable.[15]

---

[14] Watson, *op. cit.*, p. 7.

[15] Maine Annual Descriptive Report in Homemaking Education, Home Economics Branch of the Vocational Division of the Office of Education, 1958, p. 22. (Typed)

Problems of how to manage time and money effectively and how to maintain the nutritive value of foods pose a constant challenge to many homemakers. There are no readymade solutions for all families. The problem of understanding children and guiding them wisely baffles many parents and presents particular difficulties to young people who are carrying responsibilities for younger brothers and sisters and who need help as future mothers. Learning to think their way through these problems is important for these young people—both for their present and for their future lives (see also pp. 81 and 86).

A report from a Pittsburgh high school throws light on the question of whether homemaking education at the secondary level interests the intellectually gifted girl and fully utilizes her intellectual capacities. Twenty-eight girls, all but two with IQ's which ranged from 108 to 132, enrolled in a home economics class. They were tested for critical thinking and values both before and after instruction. The course dealt with the role of women; the girl and her family, present and future; family goals and values; personal and family finance; and a choice of nutrition and foods or textiles and clothing, with emphasis throughout on "understanding self and others, clarification of values, management of resources, and consumer knowledge." The course was originally planned to run a whole year, but it had to be cut to one semester in the pilot study. The tests, though not showing statistically significant differences between pre- and post-test scores, showed a clear trend toward critical thinking and an increase in "effectiveness as a family member as indicated by change in values" suggesting that a full-year course might make still more significant changes.

> The enthusiastic response of class members to the course content throughout the semester as well as the enthusiastic response of the large group at the course presentation indicates a strong feeling of need among the intellectually gifted high academic achievers for help in clarifying and coping with present and future feminine roles.[16]

There is no lack of problems in the areas of family living which are of interest to the intellectually gifted as well as to the average students. The solution of these problems constitutes a challenge to

---

[16] Anne Watkins Kozik and Irene E. McDermott, "Course for the Intellectually Gifted," *Journal of Home Economics,* Vol. 53, No. 4 (April, 1961), 266–70.

their abilities and promotes thinking on how to live intelligently as family members and as future parents.

Understanding concepts and generalizations. As solutions for problems are sought, the wise teacher helps pupils to understand the concepts involved, to perceive cause-and-effect relationships where these exist, and to generalize about such relationships. Symonds says:

> The pendulum has swung back, not into the earlier position of formal discipline, but into a belief that through the process of generalization it is possible to accomplish transfer and "mental training" on a scale not hitherto believed possible.[17]

According to Watson:

> *The best way to help pupils form a general concept is to present the concept in numerous and varied specific situations, contrasting experiences with and without the desired concept, then to encourage precise formulations of the general idea and its application in situations different from those in which the concept was learned.*[18]

A teacher from an eastern state indicates her efforts in this way:

> I tried to center in each unit a few basic principles and put these into every possible combination so that the students might discover and generalize on these principles and their use. Each year I learn and see more of the interrelationships between units taught and the principles of each. It is the principles and relationships I hoped to help pupils find and use.

A teacher in North Carolina concentrated on working out principles of management with her pupils. She had been in the community for five years and had regularly visited the farm homes of her pupils. She had observed that

> . . . many of the family kitchens were inadequate for efficient meal preparation; work centers tended to be unorganized; and much energy was used in unnecessary stooping, reaching, and walking during meal preparation.

She provided opportunity for students to study concepts of management in meal preparation, to evaluate the effectiveness of the arrangements of the large and small equipment in the school kitchen, and to work out ways in which work could be simplified.

---

[17] Symonds, *op. cit.,* p. 90.
[18] Watson, *op. cit.,* p. 7.

Then the class devised a checklist to assemble pertinent information about their home kitchens and practices and each pupil drew a floor plan of her home kitchen. These were analyzed in terms of management principles to see what improvements could be made. Class members investigated equipment and storage facilities in the school laboratory, attended a meeting on some ways to make work easier by rearranging equipment and storage in old kitchens, and made time and motion studies on meal preparation at school and at home. They rearranged some equipment and storage at school and planned and carried out some improvements at home. Parents became interested, helped to make plans, and assisted with these improvements.

The teacher found evidences that pupils had gained

> Some understanding of arrangement and organization of large equipment and small kitchen tools and supplies in relation to efficiency and comfort and pleasure in working
> More judgment in making decisions and choices
> Ability to apply understanding and judgment in planning further changes in their kitchens that they could afford
> New skills in making and improving space-saving devices for convenient storage of tools and supplies
> The habit of keeping tools and supplies where first used, and working from right to left in so far as possible, if right handed
> Some relocated furniture and equipment at home so that traffic lanes through work areas were eliminated.[19]

It is apparent that these pupils had an opportunity to learn several concepts and principles of management. Although this report does not indicate the manner in which the pupils stated these principles, it does suggest those developed. Pupils did have an opportunity not only to try out ideas at school but also to apply them in their home situations.

Team teaching at the University of Wisconsin high school has enabled seniors to gain an understanding of some important concepts in consumer economics which were not being dealt with in any one of the already existing courses. The chairman of the Business Education and Home Economics Departments planned the course in cooperation with the Social Science Department, and it

---

[19] Grace Phelps Wooton and Esther F. Segner, "Classroom Instruction Improves Home Kitchens," *Journal of Home Economics,* Vol. 50, No. 10 (December, 1958), 755–58.

has been taught by the home economics and business education teachers. The instructional responsibility is so divided that when one teaches, the other assists with preparation of materials, counsels on group and individual projects, and participates in leading class discussions.

Some of the concepts developed in this course are concerned with protection for consumers, principles of consumer buying, record keeping, budgets, income taxes, insurance and other investments, methods of buying, housing, and civic and economic responsibilities.

> In relation to protection of the consumer, two concepts emerged: (1) the consumer has the advantage of private and governmental protection, and (2) the wise consumer can gain additional financial advantage by careful selection of commodities.[20]
>
> Opportunities are given for students to become actively involved in consumer economic concerns. In 1962, members of the class had an opportunity to participate in hearings on proposed legislation geared to consumer well-being.[21]

This last example illustrates an opportunity, increasingly used, for home economics and other teachers to work together in developing and applying concepts and generalizations. As the home economics teacher involved in the consumer economics course says:

> It is clear that greater depth has been possible through this joint teaching approach, for it capitalizes on the resources of two disciplines, each of which has a unique contribution to make to consumer economic problems.[22]

A few other opportunities used by teachers for coordinating and reinforcing important learnings may be mentioned. Those pupils who have studied chemistry can more clearly understand the elements of good nutrition and the effects of cooking on the nutritive values of foods. Pupils whose study of history has given them an insight into the changes resulting from the assumption of citizenship responsibilities by individuals can more readily understand and act on their responsibility in seeing that local regulations are developed

---

[20] Rita L. Youmans, "A Course in Consumer Economics—An Experiment in Team Teaching," *Family Financial Topics for Teachers,* Vol. 10, No. 1 (Fall, 1960).

[21] Quoted from a letter to the author from Rita L. Youmans, May, 1962.

[22] Youmans, "A Course in Consumer Economics—An Experiment in Team Teaching," *op. cit.*

and enforced and that state and national legislation of importance to families is passed. The effort involved in writing interesting reports of current field trips, home, community, and club projects can help pupils to utilize their concepts of English. An understanding of ways of achieving harmony through the use of color, gained in art classes, can be applied in the choice of color schemes for clothing or home furnishing. The study in social science classes of political institutions in this and other countries can serve as a basis for understanding the contribution which individual families can make in a democracy.

Pupil Differences Affecting Learning

Meeting individual differences. The greatest challenge which teachers face in deciding on learning experiences is presented by the individual differences which exist in any class group. As indicated by Watson:

> *No two people make the same response to any school situation. Differences of heredity, physical maturity, intelligence, motor skills, health, experiences with parents, siblings, playmates; consequent attitudes, motives, drives, tastes, fears—all these and more enter into production of each individual's unique reaction. People vary in their minds and personalities as much as in their appearance.*[23]

Can the teacher who recognizes the many types of differences existing among her pupils find enough common abilities and goals to enable her to teach them as a group? According to Watson:

> *Pupils grouped by ability on any one kind of test (age, size, IQ, reading, arithmetic, science, art, music, physical fitness, and so forth) will vary over a range of several grades in other abilities and traits.* Homogeneous grouping is literally impossible except for a given limited task. On another task, a little later, these same children will not perform alike. . . . A challenging assignment . . . for one pupil may be too hard or too easy for another despite similarity in grade, age, IQ, sex, size, and school marks.[24]

The home economics teacher in Tyson Junior High School, Knoxville, Tennessee, uses the following plan to deal with the various

---

[23] Watson, *op. cit.,* p. 14.
[24] *Ibid.,* p. 15.

abilities, reading comprehension, economic levels, and home backgrounds she finds among her pupils:

> I employ a variety of methods to learn about students—school records, health records, grades, tests, observation, conferences to learn likes and dislikes, interests and attitudes toward work, home visits and conferences with mothers. After establishing rapport with pupils, we talk about goals, why we need goals, what we do with goals, what we do in order to set up our goals. The goals of individuals tend to differ but it may be possible for members of the class to be divided, for example, into those concerned with nutrition, meal preparation, consumer buying. . . . For those concerned with consumer buying, I may discuss with them such questions as: "Do you care for your sweaters yourself?" "Do you know how to care for these many kinds of sweaters?" "Do you know how to get your money's worth in sweater buying?" This may lead to a demonstration of how to select a sweater with several kinds loaned by a store.
>
> After pupils set up some of their goals, I work with pupils through a small problem to learn how to proceed with their own problems. This includes how to set up a problem, where to find information, how to set up a yardstick to work toward, how to set standards for work, why continuous evaluations help. As pupils begin work on their own problems, what each needs to learn to reach his goal is very carefully pupil-teacher planned. For example, those with the problem of buying a readymade blouse indicate why they want to work on this problem, what they need to learn more about in order to purchase a blouse that is a good buy for them. They look up basic information from books, illustrative materials, and so forth, which will help them answer such questions as: "What does the label on the blouse tell me?" "Is there enough information for me to depend on the (1) washability and (2) colorfastness? Why or why not?" "What pointers do I need to understand for good fitting in a blouse?" "Is the material suitable for the purpose it is to to be used?"
>
> I watch carefully that pupils see almost immediate results of planning so that achievement of some goals encourages them to work on long time goals. In these ways students have sufficient drive to make effective use of their own time and are able to proceed at their own rates.[25]

Dealing with or preventing undue frustration. In meeting individual differences, it is important for the teacher to be aware of the extent to which each pupil can be guided by rational purposes.

----

[25] Unpublished report supplied to author by Mrs. Dorothy White, November, 1962.

Where pupils seem unwilling or unable to set goals and carry through experiences directed toward goals, the teacher needs to ascertain the causes of the difficulty. Watson says:

> When children (or adults) experience too much frustration, their behavior ceases to be integrated, purposeful, and rational. Blindly they act out their rage or discouragement or withdrawal. The threshold of what is "too much" varies; it is lowered by previous failures.[26]

Teachers need this understanding and pupils also can learn to sense some of this truth. As one means of gaining understanding and learning to live healthfully, home economics pupils in several states carried out projects which brought them into contact with youth and adults who had special frustrations. A class of freshman home economics pupils in California became interested in a school for retarded children located across the street from their high school. They sought permission from the director of that school and from the Board of Education of the high school to assist in the care of the retarded children. Among the statement of purposes for participation sent to the Board of Education were: "To learn what causes frustration in the children and how to prevent it; to learn how children can be helped in a school for the mentally retarded." With permission from both sources, they gave parties for the children on special occasions and each day two home economics pupils assisted in the school across the street when they could be excused from class. Members of the local FHA chapter were asked to act as teachers of the retarded children while their parents were attending council meetings; they helped to staff a booth at the county fair where projects made by retarded children were displayed and in many ways assisted in creating a more understanding and acceptant attitude toward the handicapped child.[27]

A statewide project in Georgia brought some understanding of frustration and of mental health to home economics pupils in that state. State officers and advisers of the FHA, working with state specialists, set up the following objectives and suggested pertinent activities for home economics pupils:

---

[26] Watson, *op. cit.*, p. 6.
[27] Mrs. Frances L. Summers, "Bridges to Understanding," *Teen Times,* Vol. 17, No. 3 (February, 1962), 12.

To practice, as individuals, the 1-2-3's of good mental health.
To cooperate with other organizations in promoting mental health programs.
To know and use community resources in mental health.
To become acquainted with state and national mental health laws.
To become familiar with basic facts about causes and treatment of mental illness.
To develop and carry out educational and service projects in the area of mental health.

Classroom study of mental health and assembly programs which included speakers on mental health and on retardation were supplemented by such activities as making articles for patient use, contributing materials to the state hospital, taking treats to a local convalescent home, and entertaining the patients.[28]

The extent of retardation and the number of patients in mental hospitals in this country indicate how important it is for young people to come to realize that these problems are of mammoth proportions, that they may come to any family, that practicing good mental health is important for each person, and that ability to deal with difficulties may be a family problem and an important citizenship responsibility.

Any teacher may find in her classes pupils who are somewhat frustrated and who find it difficult to be rational. The bright pupil who is not sufficiently challenged or the student who has some emotional difficulties may become a behavior problem. The teacher who shares the responsibility of evaluating pupils' progress with them and with their parents finds that the pupil's realization of what is being accomplished can add appreciably to his mental health.

> A sense of progress and accomplishment encourages feelings of adequacy, independence and initiative; it maintains or increases motivation, lowers hostility and aggression stemming from frustration, and contributes to positive mental health.[29]

Slow learners who have had continuous frustrations in trying to keep up with others may be most easily upset by the school situation. When the frustrations are not severe, the teacher who is sensitive to the pupil's difficulties may help the child to overcome or adjust to the frustrations. A study of home economics teachers in

---

[28] "Guides to Action—Mental Health," *Teen Times,* Vol. 17, No. 3 (February, 1962), 11.
[29] Garry, *op. cit.,* p. 25.

Ohio, conducted by Liggett and Sellers, indicated that they had little or no training or experience in working with slow learners.[30] Bemis found that home practice was better suited to slow-learning pupils than home experiences of the type usually encouraged by home economics teachers.[31] Workshops have been organized in several states to give help on the problem of the slow learner. Whether the teacher is working with bright pupils or with slow learners, she must adjust goals and methods to their abilities and provide opportunity for experiences which fall within the range of challenge for each one and lead to satisfaction in accomplishment.

Challenging individuals. The wide differences among the backgrounds and abilities of pupils make it difficult to insure that each one will achieve his maximum growth potential. Watson's guide is pertinent:

> *The most effective effort is put forth by children when they attempt tasks which fall in the "range of challenge"—not too easy and not too hard—where success seems possible but not certain.* . . . It is not reasonable to expect a teacher to set an appropriate level of challenge for each pupil in a class; pupils can, however, learn to set their goals to bring maximum satisfaction and learning.[32]

The Tennessee and Oregon teachers' descriptions indicate how they helped pupils to set their goals and to take responsibility for achieving those goals with individuals and small groups proceeding at their own rates. Such teaching takes skill, but many teachers—recognizing that identical experiences do not mean identical learning—are seeking to help pupils become self-directive and take as much responsibility as possible for furthering their own learning and for appraising their own progress.

One teacher who had an opportunity to teach three sections of a senior course and one section of a junior course found that the students in each section differed decidedly in abilities and interests. In all sections she emphasized management and decision-making,

[30] Margaret Liggett and Beulah Sellers, "Slow Learners," *Journal of Home Economics,* Vol. 54, No. 1 (January, 1962), 23–25.

[31] Jane Bemis, "Home Experiences of Ninth and Tenth Grade Pupils of Varying Abilities" (University Park, Pa.: Ed.D. dissertation presented at Pennsylvania State University, 1958). Abstract, *Journal of Home Economics,* Vol. 52, No. 3 (March, 1960), 208–209.

[32] Watson, *op. cit.,* p. 5.

values, goals, resources, and relationships throughout the family life cycle. She found that new theories and current research stimulated the more capable students to critical thinking and to a realization of the range of alternatives possible in making a particular decision. Integration of basic principles from other courses also helped to provide depth; for example, principles learned in chemistry classes served as a springboard for understanding the problems of nutrition, while those learned in "democracy and senior science" were pertinent in solving problems of money management and housing.

For the slower learners, the teacher found it more effective to make the problems realistic by presenting a case situation of a young couple married immediately after high school graduation. Using the young man's salary and a list of the couple's expenses and desires, this group of pupils was able to make out a budget and to arrive at some important generalizations concerning the problems of buying, saving, long-range planning, management, and family relationships.[33]

Another solution to the problem of adapting teaching procedures to different types of classes and to different individuals within classes is used by many home economics teachers. They find that combining classroom, home, and club experiences facilitates meeting individual differences and adjusting tasks to the "range of challenge" found among members of most classes.

One teacher reported that during a discussion with one pupil she sensed that there was friction between the girl and a married sister who lived at home. In talking with the mother, she discovered that the sister needed maternity clothes. They agreed that the pupil needed experience in clothing construction and that they would encourage the pupil to make some clothes for the sister. The pupil was interested, the garments were made, and relations between the two sisters improved. The teacher says, "I feel this experience served as an ice breaker between the girl and her sister. Her comments to me indicate that the girl is much better emotionally because of it too."

---

[33] Taken from a typed report from a teacher in Maine, supplied to The Home Economics Education Branch, U.S. Office of Education.

Members of an FHA chapter in a senior high school in St. Petersburg, Florida were

> interested in five major problems of youth emphasized in the evaluative report prepared by FHA for the 1960 White House Conference on Children and Youth.[34] One group of senior girls took the problem of early marriage for a panel discussion at a chapter meeting. Six girls served on the panel to discuss "Early marriages, a career, or both?" Each girl chose a job for "role playing" which would present problems they had previously discussed; then, after their presentation, the listeners asked questions pertaining to the problems. The result showed the clear thinking teen-agers can do when they put their minds to the job. Said one panelist, "I actually feel as though I've had years of experience because I tried to think, act, and say what a divorced mother with three children might say as she talked to teen-agers." Another commented, "This made us think about how serious these problems of going steady and early marriages really are." [35]

It seems apparent that this and other kinds of chapter activities were a real challenge to the pupils. The teacher who effectively combines club, home, and community experiences with classroom experiences finds each often strengthens the others and that together they help to provide for individual differences.

The illustrations given in this chapter have been drawn from annual state reports, from magazines and bulletins, and from observations of and conversations with teachers during the past few years. No effort has been made to give a total picture of the program but, rather, to illustrate some of the ways in which home economics teachers are using principles of learning in teaching some aspects of home economics.

These brief sketches of ways teachers have worked with pupils suggest some do more than others in meeting individual differences. Some do a more outstanding job of challenging pupils of different abilities and backgrounds, promoting thinking, and developing and applying concepts and generalizations. Choosing a limited number of important projects and carrying them through to completion with the optimum amount of self-direction by pupils is more effective

---

[34] "Looking to the Future—A Report on the 1960 White House Conference on Children and Youth," *Teen Times,* Vol. 16, No. 1 (September, 1960), 1–17.
[35] Janet Zaia, "A Round-up of Chapter Reports on Family Fitness and Family Unity," Report from St. Petersburg, *Teen Times,* Vol. 16, No. 4 (April, 1961), 19.

than "covering the field" in home economics. With the help of discerning guidance of individuals and groups, the mental power of pupils is developed as they decide upon goals and values, recognize difficulties, consult reliable sources of information, choose promising methods of solving problems, find concepts and generalizations, apply these in other situations, and evaluate results.

CHAPTER VI

Teaching Environment and Other Aids
to Learning

One factor of importance to home economics teachers in considering a teaching position is the extent to which space and facilities make it possible to carry on the kind of home-living program which they believe may be needed. A study made by a Committee on Research in Home Economics Education of The American Vocational Association found that dissatisfaction on the part of home economics teachers is associated with inadequate equipment, especially that used for aspects other than foods and clothing. When plans for improving the equipment had been, or were being, made, with the school administrator, satisfaction was greater.[1]

As the teacher finds how many and what types of pupils are enrolled in her classes, what grade levels are represented, and what needs of youth and adults are to be met, she evaluates each aspect of the environment and its relation to what is to be taught and decides whether the school equipment is in keeping with standards attainable by families in the community. She is concerned about the atmosphere of the department, its practicality and its efficiency, as well as about its adequacy. Her questions are not unlike those the homemaker asks herself when she considers moving to a house or apartment: "In what ways is it adequate for our family?" "Does it present an attractive, inviting atmosphere to our guests?" "Must changes be made to meet needs of family members? If so. what kinds of changes?"

Some Factors to Consider in the Environment

The responsibilities of individual teachers for space and equipment vary. Some find a well-equipped home economics department

---

[1] *Factors Affecting the Satisfactions of Home Economics Teachers,* American Vocational Association Research Bulletin No. 3 (Washington, D.C.: American Vocational Association, Inc., 1948), pp. 35, 36.

which is adequate and efficiently arranged. Others find they have a responsibility to rearrange equipment and furnishings to make them more efficient and attractive, to add needed supplies or equipment, to plan how to remodel or enlarge the department so as to offer the kind of program needed, or to plan and equip a new department. In evaluating the teaching environment in a particular school, the teacher considers several factors that will affect her teaching.

Groups to be taught. Will there be pupils representing a wide variety of abilities and purposes? Is there a high dropout rate? How many pupils need vocational preparation for homemaking? Would some preparation for wage-earning vocations related to home economics be helpful? To what extent will home economics for adults be needed? What kinds of offerings will be important for them? Is the teacher expected to serve as a consultant to elementary teachers and to teach elementary pupils on occasion? Would certain additions or rearrangements facilitate achieving the purposes for these different groups?

Provisions for all phases of family living. Is there provision for teaching child development, consumer education, family and social relations, food selection and preparation, nutrition, health and safety of the family, home care of the sick, housing, home furnishing and equipment, management of family resources, and textiles and clothing?

The teaching of these different aspects of home economics, with consideration of individual differences, is facilitated by an all-purpose room (one equipped for teaching all aspects of home economics) or a multipurpose room (one equipped for teaching several aspects of home economics). Such rooms make possible individual study, group work, investigation of a variety of resource materials, and experimental and demonstration activities. All-purpose rooms have advantages—whether there is one, or more than one, teacher —since they make it possible for each teacher to carry on a broad program independently of other teachers and enable individuals and small groups to proceed at their own rates.

Some states, however, prefer multipurpose rooms to all-purpose rooms when there is more than one teacher. One room may be equipped for food preparation, meal planning, serving, meal management, nutrition, marketing, kitchen planning, and laundering. Another room may be equipped for clothing selection and construction, textiles, child development, home furnishing, family health, and home care of the sick. Management, consumer education and family-social relations may be taught in each room or in the living room. It is difficult to equip rooms in this way without giving an impression that food production and clothing construction are the major areas since the fixed equipment is likely to be for these aspects of home economics. An awareness of this difficulty can help in planning so that all aspects receive the necessary emphasis.

Attractiveness and homelikeness. Although it is important that equipment and furnishings be chosen so that they facilitate teaching and are sturdy enough for classroom use, beauty and homelikeness are important for an area of education where these are goals. These qualities can be achieved through over-all design and arrangement of equipment and furnishings, the use of color, the finishing of walls and floors, the treatment of windows, and the use of plants, flowers, and bookshelves. It is often possible to have a foyer or entrance hall to present an inviting appearance. A living room or a living-dining room helps to provide a homelike atmosphere and is particularly useful for teaching social-family relations, for discussion, for committee work, for FHA meetings, and for meetings of other groups.

Management possibilities. Is the department so organized and equipped that good management and good work habits can be developed? For example, are work areas free from traffic lanes? Are the heights of the various working surfaces satisfactory for different kinds of jobs and for pupils of different heights? Is equipment arranged so unnecessary steps are eliminated? Are supplies stored so that those used frequently are readily accessible? Do the types of equipment and furnishings represent those which families on different income levels would find it feasible to buy? (Where departments have only the most expensive and the newest models, false standards may be set and thus poor management taught.)

Bases for judgment in buying. Has the purchase of equipment and furnishings been planned so the effectiveness and efficiency of different kinds can be studied? This does not mean that large and small equipment of poor quality should be purchased. But if more than one article of a given type is needed in the department, purchasing two or more kinds can provide a basis for judging which might serve the desired purposes in different homes, particularly if a record is kept of costs, date purchased, and amounts spent for care and repair.

Health, safety, and sanitation.   Some of the important questions to consider on this point include: Is lighting adequate for pupils engaged in different kinds of activities? Is there undue glare from glossy surfaces? Are chairs comfortable for pupils of different body builds? Are the floors constructed of material which is resilient and, in the food section, water- and grease-resistant? Is electrical equipment approved by the Underwriters Laboratory? Are cleaning supplies stored for accessibility and are they protected from fire hazards?

Each of these questions on safety, management, and attractiveness can be as important to pupils as to teachers. When pupils assist in analyzing a department in relation to these factors, they are helped to discover principles they can apply in their homes.

Use of Other School and Community Facilities

What is needed in the home economics department is closely related to what is available in other parts of the school and in the community. Using other facilities may save money and space. On the other hand, duplicating or supplementing certain facilities may save time or provide a basis for evaluation of different models. For example, to provide opportunities for observation of small children, should one use the kindergartens and primary grades in the school, have a nursery school in the building, organize a play school, or depend on observation in the home? In the area of housing, pupils may learn principles of room arrangement in the department living center, the girls' lounge, or in individual projects in their homes. Houses and apartments under construction provide bases for studying types of facilities and room arrangement which may be suited to different family needs. Field trips to houses which have been or are being remodeled may suggest ways to add to convenience and attractiveness in one's own home.

Joint use of equipment and supplies by science and art teachers can enrich the work of these departments and that of the home economics department, too. It is important to decide which books, magazines, and bulletins should be kept in the school library for the general use of pupils and community members and which should be kept for study in the home economics rooms.

Remodeling or Planning a New Department

The rapid growth of the school population and the increased consolidation of schools have brought to more teachers in recent years the responsibility of assisting with the planning of home economics departments or the remodeling of older departments. This important undertaking determines the scope of the program for many years in the future and involves a substantial money investment. Fortunately there are many sources of help, including local school and community personnel, state, city, and district supervisors of home economics, state and national bulletins, and personnel in teacher education institutions and in national agencies. The wise teacher seeks help from all these sources.

Communicating with the architect. Before the architect is able to visualize the space and equipment which may be needed for home economics, he must have clearly in mind the goals which it is important to achieve and some rather concrete ideas about the way the program will be carried on. A home economics advisory committee is likely to be helpful in clarifying these ideas. A rough sketch of a possible layout may assist the architect to visualize possibilities at an early stage. Visits to other departments may help in planning arrangements and in deciding on types of storage needed. The home economics supervisor can usually suggest places to visit for specific purposes. Two criteria are of special importance in making plans: flexibility and adequate storage.

Providing for flexibility. The increase in school enrollments, the consolidation of schools, the rapid changes affecting home living, and the experimental attitudes regarding school organization demand that flexibility become a key factor in plans. Heavy, bulky, fixed, and expensive equipment should be kept to a minimum. Uncluttered open space makes a room more adjustable.

All possible means of achieving flexibility should be explored. For example, a large number of electric outlets adds to flexibility, as does the use of rubber hose connections and floor drains for sinks. Portable equipment, movable storage cabinets and partitions, adjustable shelves, and stackable chairs should be considered. What heights and sizes can be adjusted without losing stability and durability? Would interchangeable chalkboards, tackboards, and pegboards help to provide flexibility? New materials and designs should be investigated to determine what possibilities they offer for adjusting to different teaching requirements.

Planning for adequate storage. Unless the rooms are unduly large, which makes for difficult teaching, some of the equipment will have to be kept in storage part of the time. An exact list of such items will enable the architect to plan space so that each is easy to get at as well as easy to keep clean and in order. Dividing aspects of home economics into those which are likely to be studied at the same time and those which will be studied only at certain times during the year will help to clarify storage needs.

Examples of items and equipment for which storage usually needs to be planned are: reference books, educational pamphlets, magazines, charts, posters, folders for pupil records, folders for clippings for pupil and teacher use, photographs, and samples of products to be analyzed (e.g., swatches of different fabrics, different grades of canned goods, steps in a construction process, different kinds of appliances, accessories, and furnishings, ready-to-wear garments of various qualities and designs, toys and games for children). Some states have checklists of items for individual, small-group, and occasional use.

Not only the kind but also the organization of storage space is important. Can different kinds of items be stored so that each is visible and can be removed without having to move another? What filing system will make it easy to find and replace the various items? Where should different articles be placed so they are convenient to the point of first use? Will dividers in drawers be useful in holding small articles in place? What articles should be hung so each is within easy reach? Are items often used within easy access of the majority of persons using them?

The number and kinds of items to be stored will determine whether it is advisable to have a separate storage room for large equipment, a storage closet, cabinets built along the wall of the homemaking room, or all of these.

Choosing and Using Learning Aids

Besides the equipment and supplies which are provided for teaching home economics, other types of learning aids—if selected carefully and used properly—can help pupils achieve their goals. The many types of experiences which are a natural part of the program need to be chosen with clearly defined goals in mind. For example, are pupils learning to do, to think, and to feel in ways that are important in modern living? Are they becoming aware of concepts and generalizations which will help them in new situations? Are they able to recognize assumptions, made or implied, and to draw inferences from data?

Although pupils can make excellent suggestions for the kinds of experiences which will help them to attain goals in which they are interested, most pupils need careful guidance in preparing for, carrying through, and analyzing an experience so as to discover its deeper meaning.

Resource materials. Textbooks, reference books, bulletins, charts, tables, samples, and pictorial materials provide a basis for gathering facts to use in diagnosing situations and solving problems. Several books by different authors covering similar subject matter and adapted to different reading levels aid in the thorough consideration of a topic. What are the facts presented? What are areas of agreement or disagreement? Has there been recent research which throws light on the questions under discussion? In a society in which research is constantly adding to knowledge and advertising is a daily pressure, it is important that pupils learn to read with discrimination. Do some pupils need help in using reference materials (for example, an index, a table of contents, a card file, a reader's guide) more efficiently, or in summarizing?

Can pupils put into chart or table form such data as the incidence of children's diseases over a period of years, the cost of certain foods in different seasons, the growth of rats fed different diets? Do they know how to draw justified conclusions from a chart or table? Do they see limitations in the data? Do they consider the representativeness of samples before drawing conclusions? Do they need to see each step in a construction process, or can they analyze the completed product and determine how it was made?

Laboratory experiences. Using facilities in a well-equipped department wisely can contribute to different types of objectives. Experiences in the school laboratory, in the home, and in the community are all important for home economics pupils. For example, experiments with procedures and products can bring out principles basic to buying, to cooking, to laundering, to management, and to beauty in arrangements. Pupils can discover what quality of fabric or of food is desirable for different purposes, whether a given temperature is needed for cooking all proteins, whether woven and knitted garments of the same fibers are laundered in the same way, what short cuts save time and energy and produce a satisfactory result, how one organizes meal preparation so that all dishes are ready at the same time, how color affects the feeling of unity, what variations in initiative are shown by different children, which appliances are easiest to care for and use.

After a pupil has gained an understanding of these concepts, generalizations, and principles, he should try them out at home or in a community project in order to discover wider applications of them. If skill is desired, it is important to understand why certain techniques are useful, to try out the steps to check one's understanding and ability to follow the procedures, and then to repeat the process (usually at home) until some facility is attained. A clarification of the purposes for each laboratory experience will help teacher and pupils check how many and what type are needed by pupils at different stages in their development.

Visual experiences. As a supplement to, or as preparation for, a laboratory experience, many pupils find it desirable to see a process carried on through a demonstration, on a field trip, or through watching a film or film strip. Realization of different personal and family values can often be clearly seen in a film, the setting for family and social relations questions presented in a film which is stopped at a crucial point is a helpful basis for discussion, a visit to a kindergarten can reveal interesting adult-child relationships, an understanding of principles can be gained and skillful techniques seen in a demonstration.

The preparation for the experience and the analysis of it afterward determine the real values of the experience. Preparation for the experience will involve making decisions regarding the purposes to be served, the questions to be answered, the extent to which all pupils will get answers to the same questions or to different ones, the basic reading to be done, and whether or not pupils will identify with different people in the film or on the field trip. If the field situation is complex, a preliminary conference may be needed to arrange for elimination of all but pertinent elements.

The analysis following the experience is as important as the preparation. It will be facilitated if each pupil forms the habit of writing down a brief summary of his observations and a list of the most important ideas he has gained. These discussions provide opportunity to define principles, to clear up misunderstandings, and to determine whether or not the purposes have been achieved.

These few types of learning experiences serve only to indicate the necessity of choosing those which are most pertinent and the importance of so preparing for them and analyzing them that the purposes are attained and optimum results secured.

The home economics department with its equipment, supplies, and other learning aids can be a rich source of experiences for pupils. But these experiences must be supplemented by experiences in the home and in the community to give breadth and depth of understanding. Each part of the environment and each type of learning experience and resource material should be so chosen and used that it enriches the learner and contributes fundamentally to the purposes of the program.

CHAPTER VII

The Preparation of the Teacher

The student preparing to teach home economics in the secondary school needs a background which will not only enable her to help develop pupils' abilities and understandings in home and family life, but one which will also help her to live richly as an informed and effective individual and as a citizen of the community. Unfortunately there are not adequate terms to refer to these aspects of her education. *General education* and *professional education* cannot be accurately applied to different subjects. By the same token, the alleged distinctions between liberal and technical education are misleading since "liberal education may be utilitarian as well as of enduring value for its own sake. Technical education may be liberal as well as utilitarian." [1] Nevertheless these terms continue to be used in reference to college programs and are used here for convenience.

Another practice in common use and followed here is that of designating titles of courses to be included as general and professional education. It is common knowledge that a course of a given title often varies widely in content and presentation among different institutions and even among faculty members of the same department. A sounder procedure, followed by several institutions, is that of deciding upon purposes to be served and then choosing or developing courses which achieve these purposes.

Initial Preparation

Since the early 1920's the usual practice has been to provide a four-year preservice preparation for home economics teachers, with the understanding that this would be supplemented by in-service education on the job, summer school courses, and other graduate offerings. A few states require five years of preparation; others require successive periods of study beyond the bachelor's degree.

---

[1] T. M. Stinnett, *The Profession of Teaching* (Washington, D.C.: The Center for Applied Research in Education, Inc., 1962), p. 92.

Some states are requiring periodic professional improvement for certificate renewal, instead of issuing permanent certificates. These practices are a recognition of the accelerating rate of change in society and of the vast accumulation of knowledge—two developments which have made education more than ever a lifetime process.

In thinking of the general education part of the teacher's preparation, most home economics staff members seek courses which "stretch the mind, enliven the imagination, develop the powers and sensitiveness of students" [2] and deal directly with "such matters of common concern as local and national political affairs, developments on the international scene, the making of a home and the rearing of a family, acquiring and engaging in recreational activities which enrich and stabilize life." [3] While seeking such courses, home economics staff members must also decide how they will teach their own courses so as to contribute to general as well as professional purposes and whether their responsibility is confined to home economics students or whether they should make a significant contribution to other students in the common concern of "the making of a home and the rearing of a family."

In planning for the professional part of the prospective teacher's program, the staff must decide what supporting sciences and arts are needed as well as what aspects of home economics and what kind of education courses serve the purposes which are important to the future teacher. What concepts and principles should be understood, for example, in family relations and human development? in consumption and family economics? in management? in maintenance of health? What skills are needed for satisfying home living today? What attitudes and appreciations may be significant? How can students be given opportunity for acquiring an understanding of pupils in different stages of their development? of the educational process and principles of learning? of the place of the school in a changing society? How can skill be developed in translating these understandings through practice in the teaching of the various

---

[2] Lewis Webster Jones, "The Challenge of Home Economics Within a Framework of a Liberal Education," *Proceedings of the American Association of Land-Grant Colleges and State Universities, 1957* (Washington, D.C.: The Association, 1957), p. 294.

[3] Earl J. McGrath, "The Ideal Education of the Professional Man," in *Education for the Professions,* Sixty-First Yearbook of the National Society for the Study of Education, Part II (Chicago: The University of Chicago Press, 1962), p. 292.

aspects of home economics and in the maintenance of satisfactory relations with parents and with community agencies and organizations?

Purposes for home economics students. As college faculties state the purposes for home economics students, they may first state the total goals as a guide for general and professional education:

As outcomes of the four-year undergraduate curriculum in the Division of Home Economics it is hoped that students will continue to: acquire knowledge; develop understandings; develop ability in critical thinking and creativity; develop attitudes, interests and appreciations; and, develop skills and habits involved in:

*1. Establishing and maintaining a home which contributes effectively to furthering individual and family well-being.

*2. Establishing and maintaining satisfying human relationships.

*3. Clarifying and using values and goals as guides for satisfying personal, family and professional living.

*4. Contributing to the optimum mental and physical health for self and others.

**5. Expressing one's thoughts clearly in speaking and writing and intelligently interpreting one's reading, listening to and viewing a variety of materials.

**6. Enjoying literature, music, art and other cultural activities as expressions of personal and social experiences and participating to some extent in some form of creative activity for the enrichment of living.

**7. Understanding the physical world, applying habits of scientific thought to personal and civic problems, and appreciating the meaning of scientific discoveries in relation to human welfare.

**8. Participating as an informed and responsible citizen in solving the social, economic, and political problems of the local, national, and world community.

***9. Becoming oriented professionally and preparing for a career in harmony with personal resources and social needs.

It is recognized that there is desirable overlapping and no sharp lines between the three categories; . . . however, they are classified as follows:

* Major objectives which apply to common requirements in home economics.

** Major objectives which apply to general education.

*** Major objective for professional education.[4]

---

[4] "Progress Report on the New Undergraduate Curriculum" (Stillwater, Okla.: Division of Home Economics, Oklahoma State University, 1963), p. 4. Mimeographed. See also statements of goals by Committee on Criteria for Evaluation of College Programs in Home Economics, *Home Economics in Higher Education* (Washington, D.C.: American Home Economics Association, 1949), pp. 26–88.

Programs for Home Economics Teachers

A variety of plans for the organization of programs has been used in efforts to provide opportunity for prospective home economics teachers to achieve goals thought to be important. Not all of these plans have been completely satisfactory and experimentation continues. One plan frequently used is that of setting up one or more courses in each of the aspects of home economics discussed in Chapter IV. This is likely to result in a number of introductory courses of little depth. Usually more courses have been included in foods and clothing than in other areas; this has meant too little preparation in other important aspects. Traditionally, there have been such heavy requirements in the physical and biological sciences that the social sciences and the humanities have had insufficient attention. Many programs have been so rigidly organized that individual interests and capacities could not be met. Efforts are being made to overcome these difficulties.

Plans for teacher preparation in two institutions illustrate some ways to overcome certain of these difficulties. Different institution practices have to be kept in mind in order to get the full picture— the use of quarter or semester credits, the use of special "general education" courses or courses serving both general education and preprofessional education purposes, the requiring of specific home economics and supporting courses or allowing opportunity for choice, the requiring of a minor in addition to a major in home economics for prospective teachers.

One illustration. Institution A is set up on the quarter plan with 192 quarter credits for graduation. Specific general education courses required of all college students total forty-eight credit hours and include: natural science (twelve), social science (twelve), humanities (twelve), American thought and language (nine), health, physical education, and recreation (three). No decision has yet been reached by the home economics staff regarding the contribution of home economics to the general education of nonmajors.

The preprofessional and supporting courses for home economics teachers provide for a choice between chemistry (twelve hours beyond the natural science requirement) or courses selected from sociology, psychology, philosophy, political science, and social work (20 hours beyond the social science requirement).

The home economics includes fifteen hours which all home economics majors take: nutrition for man (three), design for living (three), human development in the family (three), management principles (three), senior seminar (three). In addition, prospective teachers take thirty-five to forty credit hours in meal management (five), home management residence (four), family finance (three), child study (four), the consumer in the market (three), interpersonal relations in the home or understanding family living (three), principles of clothing construction (three), housing and home furnishing (four), selection of clothing for the family (three), and also advanced nutrition (five) if chemistry had been chosen.

The professional education hours total thirty-two to thirty-eight and include the individual and the school (six), school and society (six), methods of teaching and student teaching in home economics (eighteen), and a seminar in home economics education (two to eight).[5] All home economics teachers are required to have a teaching minor of thirty hours. For certain minors some of the preprofessional and professional courses count as both major and minor credits. For example, if the minor is in physical science, thirteen of the hours taken in the option with chemistry count also as a part of the minor, which with three more in chemistry, four in natural science, and twelve in mathematics, physics, or geology leaves twenty-nine free elective hours which may enable the student to broaden or deepen her preparation.[6]

Another pattern. Curriculum study by Institution B resulted in somewhat different choices. There, 135 semester credits are required for graduation. Instead of certain "general education" courses required of all college students, home economics prospective teachers take forty-nine hours in courses which serve both general education purposes and as supporting courses for home economics. These include anthropology (three), the arts and humanities (nine), English and speech (fifteen), bacteriology (three), chemistry (six), history (three), psychology (three), health and physical education (four), and a choice of six credits from sociology, anthropology, economics, or government and politics.

[5] Rosalind Mentzer, *A Report of the Process Used in Revising Curriculum in the College of Home Economics* (East Lansing, Michigan: College of Home Economics, 1962), 26 pp.

[6] Mentzer, From typed and mimeographed material in letter to author, December 18, 1962.

Home economics courses for teachers include a total of fifty-four credits, eighteen of which are required of all home economics majors: development in the family (three), textiles and dress in modern living (three), food and people (three), communities and families (three), decision-making in family living (three), space for family living (three). These courses are available to all college students as well as being required for home economics students. The emphasis is "upon the social significance of several aspects of family life . . . physiological and psychological significance, economic and political significance, in many different cultures and many periods of history." [7]

Professional courses in home economics required beyond the eighteen semester hours of common requirements total twenty-two hours and include child development (four), family relationships (three), clothing selection (three), nutrition of the family (three), family financial planning (three), home management experience (three), and household equipment (three). In addition to these forty credits, prospective teachers choose fourteen credit hours in one of three areas. One provides further depth in the area of the family and includes child development (five), foundations of marriage (three), family health (one), home planning (five). Another includes clothing construction (six), foods and family meals (five), family health (one), and home arts (two). The third provides for greater depth in family finance and includes elementary textiles (two), home planning (three), household buying (three), managing family financial resources or economic conditions in relation to the family (three), and principles of marketing (three), with supporting courses chosen from economics.

The education courses in this institution total twenty-four semester hours and include education in American society (three), educational psychology (three), and home economics education, including student teaching where curriculum and methods in home economics are considered.

Translating credit hours into percentages makes apparent some differences in emphasis in the two programs. The eight hours of electives in Institution B are extended by the options for fourteen

---

[7] Grace M. Henderson, "Education and Family Professional Services" (University Park, Pa.: College of Home Economics, Pennsylvania State University, 1962), p. 13. Mimeographed.

credits in home economics. In Institution A electives may be increased by the choice of a minor. Institution B makes available to all college students eighteen semester hours of home economics as a contribution to general education. In Institution A no decision has been made about this. Thirty-five per cent of the credits are devoted to general education in Institution A and 6 to 10 per cent to supporting courses, a total of 41–45 per cent; in Institution B, the two together constitute 36 per cent of the credits. The relative proportion in home economics differs, being 26 per cent to 29 per cent in Institution A, and 40 per cent in Institution B. In both there is less emphasis on food and clothing skills and more on child development, family relations, management, and family finance than was formerly true. A rough tabulation would show the following:

INSTITUTION A (192 quarter credits)	Per cent	INSTITUTION B (135 semester credits)	Per cent
General education requirements:	35	General and supporting courses:	36
American language, 9; natural science, 12; social science, 12; humanities, 12; physical education, 3.		anthropology, 3; arts and humanities, 9; English and speech, 15; bacteriology, 3; chemistry, 6; history, 3; psychology, 3; physical education, 4; and sociology, anthropology, economics, or government and politics, 6.	
Supporting courses:	6–10		
chemistry, 12; or sociology, philosophy, political science, or social work, 20.			
Home economics:	26–29	Home economics:	40
art, 3; child study and family living, 10; management, 7; house and furnishing, 4; clothing and textiles, 9; family finance and consumption, 6; nutrition and meals, 8–13; senior seminar, 3.		child development and family relations, 13; clothing selection and textiles, 6; food and nutrition, 6; management, 9; house furnishing and equipment, 6; and family living, family finance, or home skills, 14.	
Education	16–20	Education	18
Minor teaching field	15		
Electives	2 +	Electives	6

A third proposal. A somewhat different plan may well merit further study. This allows for a limited number of common requirements and professional courses in home economics with further concentration in one of three types of supporting areas and the related areas of home economics. The common requirements in home economics include ten to twelve semester credits in management and human development, followed by twenty to twenty-two credits in child development (three), family relations (three), clothing and textiles (four), family economics (three), food and nutrition (four), the house, its furnishings and equipment (three).

The method of getting concentration beyond this varies, depending upon the institution's plan for general education. Where certain general education courses are required of all students, the supporting courses chosen must be beyond these. If there is flexibility in choice of general education courses, concentration takes the place of general education in one area, while general education courses are taken in the other areas. For example, students wishing to build strength in the social sciences take the general education courses in the natural sciences, the humanities, and the arts. They take needed courses in economics, sociology, anthropology, and/or psychology as background for further study in family economics, management, child development, and family relations. Students concentrating in the natural sciences take more advanced courses in food and nutrition, health, housing, equipment, and textiles, and general education courses in the social sciences and the humanities. Or, those concentrating in the humanities may build strength in the arts and the historical aspects of clothing, housing, home furnishing, and textiles.

Each of the three plans has some advantages, providing more depth in areas especially important in modern home living, less rigidity than earlier plans, and greater provision for individual differences. Each also demands time for counseling with students. Some preparation in the various aspects of home economics to be taught is important and depth in some is desirable. School administrators and supervisors have a responsibility for making a place in the schools for teachers well prepared in some of these less traditional phases of home economics. Because college faculties are accepting the responsibility for continuous curriculum study and evaluation, modifications in such patterns as have been illustrated will occur as more data accumulate about their usefulness.

Professional education.   There are many aspects of education which might be included in the student's program. Among these are its historical, psychological, social, and philosophical aspects. As in the case of preparation in the subject speciality, a four- or even a five-year program does not allow for strong preparation in all the areas which might be desirable. Some of them, fortunately, are more meaningful after experience in the profession. The two institutions whose courses were listed apparently give prospective teachers some background for understanding pupils through courses on the individual and the school, or on educational psychology. They also provide a basis for understanding the place of the school in modern society through the courses on school and society or education in American society.

The home economics education curriculum and methods courses building on these help students to analyze the needs of adolescents in the areas of home living, to gain ability to organize and provide home economics programs in junior and senior high school for pupils with different abilities and purposes, and to work with parents and community agencies. Developing the ability to make the day-to-day decisions wisely on the basis of principles requires time and wise guidance. The home economics curriculum and methods courses in which concepts and generalizations are developed may precede or coincide with student teaching. These courses are sometimes followed by a seminar to make possible an understanding of the wider application of principles.

Student teaching in home economics has, for some years, involved the use of off-campus centers where the student can have experience in the teacher's full-day program and can live in the community and concentrate on learning to teach home economics without being enrolled in other college courses. It is important that the prospective teacher have experience in teaching different phases of home economics and in carrying other school and community responsibilities. The time allotted for student teaching varies, though six weeks to half a semester has been usual. The amount of time needed by individuals varies widely.

A well-prepared supervising teacher with a strong home economics program can work with the college methods teacher in coordinating the learning from education, home economics education, and student teaching. For example, the adaptation of principles of learning in child development and family relations requires judgment and skill somewhat different from that needed in nutrition and in food preparation. Working with a full class requires abilities somewhat different from those required in working with small groups and individuals. Challenging the gifted or guiding the slow learner in the area of financial management calls for particular teaching abilities, as does leading an FHA group, teaching a class, or making a home visit.

Making the myriad of day-to-day decisions with pupils demands a quality of teacher education which cannot be acquired in a short time. In-service education can build on the college experience and strengthen it in many ways.

Continuing Education

Teaching, like other professions, depends for much of its effectiveness on continued learning. Many opportunities are available. Home economics supervisors and school administrators—through local, district, and state conferences; curriculum study; individual visits; newsletters; and action research—help in pointing the way to the solution of many problems. Graduate study enables the teacher to get more depth and/or breadth in her preparation. Travel, exchange programs with other countries, and foreign service or study can contribute much to the home economics teacher. Active participation in professional and lay organizations provides many opportunities for personal growth. The alert teacher will take advantage of these and seek other means of continuing education.

Preparing for the profession of teaching home economics provides the undergraduate college student with the opportunity to acquire a general education in the sciences and the humanities and an education focused on two of the most influential institutions in society: the home and the school, both of which so profoundly affect individuals. Preparation for this profession in a democratic and changing society demands emphasis on current, not outmoded, types of problems. It requires developing concepts, generalizations, attitudes, and appreciations likely to serve in new home situations. It demands a program which allows for enough flexibility to meet individual differences in background, interests, and capacities.

The home is the focal point—the nucleus—of every society. It has been said: "When you educate a man, you educate an individual; when you educate a woman, you educate a whole family." As situations in the home change, this may no longer be true. Any educator in the field of home economics, however, whether teaching men or women, has a major opportunity in this cradle of individuality and culture. To make use of this opportunity, absorbs all the learning, experience, and creativity which a person can command and apply.

Bibliography

GENERAL REFERENCES

Bloom, Benjamin S. (Ed.), *Taxonomy of Educational Objectives.* New York: David McKay Co., Inc., 1956.

Committee on Philosophy and Objectives of Home Economics, *Home Economics—New Directions.* Washington, D.C.: American Home Economics Association, 1959.

Hall, Olive A. and Beatrice Paolucci, *Teaching Home Economics.* New York: John Wiley & Sons, Inc., 1961.

Hatcher, Hazel M. and Mildred E. Andrews, *The Teaching of Home Economics,* 2nd ed. Boston: Houghton Mifflin Company, 1963.

Hunt, Caroline L., *The Life of Ellen H. Richards, 1842–1911.* Washington, D.C.: American Home Economics Association, 1942.

Williamson, Maude and Mary Stewart Lyle, *Homemaking Education in the High School,* 4th ed. New York: Appleton-Century-Crofts, Inc., 1961.

CURRICULUM

Balance in the Curriculum, 1961 Yearbook of the Association for Supervision and Curriculum Development. Washington, D.C.: National Education Association, 1961.

Douglass, Harl R., *Trends and Issues in Secondary Education.* Washington, D.C.: The Center for Applied Research in Education, Inc., 1962.

French, Will and Associates, *Behavioral Goals of General Education in High School.* New York: Russell Sage Foundation, 1957.

Stratemeyer, Florence B., Margaret G. McKim, and Mayme Sweet, *Guides to a Curriculum for Modern Living.* New York: Teachers College, Bureau of Publications, Columbia University, 1952.

Tyler, Ralph W., *Basic Principles of Curriculum and Instruction.* Chicago: The University of Chicago Press, 1950.

Vocational Education in the Years Ahead, Chapter VI: "Homemaking Education." U.S. Office of Education, Division of Vocational Education, Bulletin No. 234. Washington, D.C.: USGPO, 1945.

EQUIPMENT AND OTHER LEARNING AIDS

Bachman, John W., *How to Use Audio-Visual Materials.* New York: Association Press, 1956.

Dale, Edgar, *Audio-Visual Methods in Teaching.* New York: The Dryden Press, 1954.

East, Marjorie, *Display for Learning*. New York: The Dryden Press, 1952.

Lee, Ata, *Space and Equipment for Homemaking Programs*. U.S. Office of Education, Division of Vocational Education, Misc. No. 9. Washington, D.C.: USGPO, 1950.

Schooler, Ruth and Mary Mather, "Planning Homemaking Departments," *Illinois Teacher of Home Economics*, Vol. IV, No. 7 (1961), 296–342.

Walker, Beulah and Mary Mather, "Innovations in Space and Facilities for Homemaking Departments," *Illinois Teacher of Home Economics*, Vol. V, No. 5 (1962), 195–240.

Wendt, Paul R., *Audio-Visual Instruction*. Washington, D.C.: National Education Association, 1957.

LEARNING PROCESS

Burton, William H., Roland B. Kimball, and Richard L. Wing, *Education for Effective Thinking*. New York: Appleton-Century-Crofts, Inc., 1960.

Garry, Ralph, *The Psychology of Learning*. Washington, D.C.: The Center for Applied Research in Education, Inc., 1963.

Prescott, Daniel A., *The Child in the Educative Process*. New York: McGraw-Hill Book Company, Inc., 1957.

Prescott, Daniel A., *Factors that Influence Learning*. Pittsburgh, Pa.: University of Pittsburgh Press, 1958.

Symonds, Percival M., *What Education Has to Learn from Psychology*, 2nd ed. New York: Teachers College, Bureau of Publications, Columbia University, 1959.

Watson, Goodwin, *What Psychology Can We Trust?* New York: Teachers College, Bureau of Publications, Columbia University, 1961.

TEACHER EDUCATION

Committee on Criteria for Evaluation of College Programs in Home Economics, *Home Economics in Higher Education*. Washington, D.C.: American Home Economics Association, 1949.

Coon, Beulah I., *Home Economics in Colleges and Universities of the United States*, Federal Security Agency, Home Economics Education Series No. 26. Washington, D.C.: USGPO, n.d.

National Commission on Teacher Education and Professional Standards, *New Horizons: The Becoming Journey*. Washington, D.C.: National Education Association, 1962.

———, *The Education of Teachers—Certification*. Washington, D.C.: National Education Association, 1961.

———, *The Education of Teachers—Curriculum Programs*. Washington, D.C.: National Education Association, 1959.

Stinnett, T. M., *The Profession of Teaching*. Washington, D.C.: The Center for Applied Research in Education, Inc., 1962.

Woodruff, Asahel D., *Basic Concepts of Teaching with Brief Readings*, Parts I and II. San Francisco: Chandler Publishing Company, 1962.

Index